A BIBLIOGRAPHY AND NOTES ON THE WORKS OF
LASCELLES ABERCROMBIE

Lascelles Abercrombie, c. 1919.

A Bibliography and Notes on the Works of
LASCELLES ABERCROMBIE

by
JEFFREY COOPER

KAYE & WARD LTD
LONDON

Published by
Kaye & Ward Ltd
194–200 Bishopsgate, London E.C.2
1969

SBN 7182 0770 X

Printed in England by
Adlard & Son Limited
Bartholomew Press, Dorking

IN MEMORY OF RALPH ABERCROMBIE

LASCELLES ABERCROMBIE

Born: Ashton-upon-Mersey, Cheshire; January 9, 1881.

Married: Grange-over-Sands, Lancs.; January 23, 1909.

Died: London; October 27, 1938.

CONTENTS

ILLUSTRATIONS

PREFACE

In this bibliography an attempt has been made to cover the subject as widely and completely as possible. It is hoped that such calculated omissions as there are do not detract from the value of the work. Contributions to anthologies, for example, have been excluded except where they are of special interest or significance. An attempt was made to trace the examination papers compiled by L. A. Although the relevant universities cooperated to the utmost, so few details were found that the inclusion of them would be of very little interest. The few private letters that have been published will be noted against the books in the acknowledgement section, but are not included in the body of the bibliography.

The innumerable written reports, speeches and lectures have been excluded; a bibliography is no place for them. However, if lectures were published *in toto*, these are included. It is my opinion that the variant bindings of *Interludes and Poems* (red buckram) and *Speculative Dialogues* (pink buckram), originally owned by Lord Esher, are just re-bindings from the ordinary bindings. This opinion is supported by John Hayward in *English Poetry* (National Book League, 1950).

All known performances of plays are included, but if they were read by L. A. to an audience, they are not.

In contributions to books, later impressions of the first edition are omitted completely; later editions are just noted. Annual publications are entered under periodicals; bi-annuals and tri-annuals, etc. are entered under contributions to books.

I hope I will be forgiven by those who dislike the idea of listing 'definite', 'probable', and 'possible' contributions together. I should not like to think that because such a system is used doubt could be cast on the dependability of other items.

The original prices of the editions of principal books, where known, are given after the publication dates. All principal books bound together with other books, whether by L. A. or not, are listed under principal books. Cross-referencing has been included as much as possible to save constant reference to the index; it also leads to better clarification. Numbers in brackets referring to cross-references are item numbers. Format sizes are to the nearest eighth of an inch. All items that have not been personally examined are denoted by an asterisk next to the item number.

Although I have attempted to make this bibliography as full and accurate as possible, there are obviously mistakes and omissions. For all these I accept any blame, but would ask that if anyone knows of any corrections or additions, he or she would please advise me of them, via the publisher.

The main body of poetry and fictional prose manuscripts were given by Mrs Abercrombie to the Brotherton Library, University of Leeds, in January, 1948.

Some were given to the Bodleian Library, Oxford, in 1939 by Mr Percy Withers. There are probably a few scattered among unknown people. Those remaining in the hands of the Abercrombie family are mainly lecture notes and copies of poems in his hand.

I would like to acknowledge my extreme gratitude to the following for helping me clarify certain aspects of this bibliography.

David Abercrombie; Michael Abercrombie; Mr R. F. Bisson; the British Broadcasting Corporation; Mrs Daisy Kennedy Drinkwater; Mrs Jan Marsh; Mrs Joy Masefield; Mr M. Rao, Education department, the High Commission of India in London; Mr Martin Secker; the United Arab Republic Cultural Counsellor in London; and Mrs Jessie Vickars-Gaskell.

To Julian Trevelyan for showing me the collection of letters written by L. A. to Robert Trevelyan. To Miss Monica Withers for showing me the collection of letters L. A. wrote to Percy Withers, and other material. A few miscellaneous letters were made available to me from other people mentioned.

The libraries I found to be extremely useful, if not invaluable, were: The British Museum (Bloomsbury and Colindale); the London Library; the City of Liverpool Library; the University of London Library; and Birkbeck College (the Robert Trevelyan Library), University of London.

I obtained help from the majority of publishers I contacted, and to them I express my thanks.

The following books and articles proved to be most helpful (all published in London, unless otherwise stated).

Ten Contemporaries, by John Gawsworth (Ernest Benn; 1932)

'Lascelles Abercrombie', by Oliver Elton (with Percy Withers and Ralph Abercrombie) (*Proceedings of the British Academy,* Vol. XXV; 1939)

A Number of People, by Edward Marsh (Heinemann, and Hamilton; 1939)

'Lascelles Abercrombie as I knew him', by Percy Withers (*English,* Vol. IV, No. 24; Autumn, 1943)

[This article contains extracts from some letters L. A. wrote Percy Withers.]

Edward Marsh, by Christopher Hassell (Longmans; 1959)

Rupert Brooke, by Christopher Hassell (Faber and Faber; 1964)

The Georgian Revolt, by Robert H. Ross (Carbondale and Edwardsville: Southern Illinois University Press; 1965)

[This book contains extracts from some letters by L. A. to Edward Marsh.]

Lastly, I have to acknowledge the untiring help of both Mrs Catherine Abercrombie and the late Ralph Abercrombie. Mrs Abercrombie gave me access to all her letters, her collection of books, and herself for many hours of discussion, from which I gained invaluable information. To Ralph Abercrombie I am more than grateful, for he gave me all the assistance he could from his wide knowledge of this subject, together with the use of his collection of articles, books, and other miscellaneous material. Without either, this bibliography would have been far from complete, and may not have got past the first outline.

J. C.

PRINCIPAL BOOKS, ETC

Interludes and Poems
Mary and the Bramble
The Sale of Saint Thomas [Act 1]
Emblems of Love
Thomas Hardy
Deborah
Speculative Dialogues
Poetry and Contemporary Speech
The Epic
An Essay Towards a Theory of Art
Four Short Plays
Principles of English Prosody
Phoenix
Stratford-upon-Avon Report
The Theory of Poetry
The Idea of Great Poetry
Romanticism
Twelve Idyls and Other Poems
Progress in Literature
The Poems of Lascelles Abercrombie
The Sale of Saint Thomas
Principles of Literary Criticism
Poetry: Its Music and Meaning
To Sir Walford Davies
Lyrics and Unfinished Poems
The Art of Wordsworth
Vision and Love

---

(1)   INTERLUDES AND POEMS

First edition:

1908   *INTERLUDES | AND POEMS | BY LASCELLES ABERCROMBIE | LONDON: JOHN LANE, THE BODLEY HEAD | NEW YORK: JOHN LANE COMPANY. MCMVIII*

Format: Crown 8vo, $7\frac{1}{2} \times 4\frac{3}{4}$ ins.

Collation: 176 pages, consisting of:—
half-title, verso blank (pp. 1-2); title page, imprint on verso (pp. 3-4); dedication [*To Catherine*], verso blank (pp. 5-6); *Contents*, verso blank (pp. 7-8); fly-title [*The New God: A Miracle*], verso blank (pp. 9-10); pages 11-174, text; acknowledgements, verso blank (pp. 175-176).

Binding: green cloth; gilt lettering on spine; blind impression of single-line border on front and outside back covers; white end papers; top edges of leaves gilt; fore and lower edges uncut. A second binding state, c. 1910, has the following differences: 1. the spine of the second state is rounded, where the original is flat; 2. binding tape is used in the original, but not in the second state.

Signatures: A^8 B–L^8

Publication Date: January 29, 1908 [5s.]

Contents: INTERLUDES.

The New God: A Miracle (page 11)

> A dramatic poem of 578 lines; it is not known when it was written, but it was definitely before August, 1906 when he sent it to G. Lowes Dickinson with 'Blind'. Although he thought this one of the best poems in this book, it was refused by every periodical he sent it to.

Blind (page 39)

> A dramatic poem of 679 lines; it was probably written in 1906. Originally called 'Blind Hatred', it was to have been changed to 'The Prodigal Father', but was reduced simply to 'Blind'. On January 7, 1907 he received confirmation that it was to be published in the *Independent Review*, q.v. (**254**), making it the first poem of his to be published in a well-known London periodical. It was revised slightly from 676 lines in the *Independent Review* for inclusion in this collection.
>
> In July, 1907, Grant Allen of London suggested putting this on the stage, but although all arrangements had been made by L. A., including revising to make it more actable, it was not, after all, staged.

The Fool's Adventure (page 71)

> A dramatic poem divided into four parts, with lines: part I, 137; II, 194; III, 185; IV, 74. It is not known when it was written, but certainly before June 19, 1907.

An Escape (page 99)

> A dramatic poem of 618 lines; definitely finished writing before June 19, 1907.

Peregrinus (page 127)

> A dramatic poem of 595 lines; probably originally written in 1906, he began to revise it for this book on November 23, 1907. The revising was finished on December 13, 1907, and although he was not very satisfied with it, it was sent straight to Lane without any further revision.

Soul and Body (page 155)

A dramatic poem of 63 lines. On November 20, 1907, he received a letter from the *Nation* requesting a specimen of poetry. He wrote this the same day, revising and correcting some points the following day. It was later published in the *Nation*, q.v. (**547**).

The Trance (page 158)

A poem of 49 lines. Written for the *Nation* on December 5, 1907; he was not very satisfied with it, especially the ending, which he tried to correct while going over the proofs. It was later published in the *Nation*, q.v. (**548**)

Ceremonial Ode (Intended For A University) (page 161)

A poem in three stanzas, 33 lines. Written on June 9, 1907, it was originally called 'Ode Written for Manchester University', but was never published as such.

'All Last Night . . .' (page 163)

A poem of 16 lines, four stanzas; written in November, 1905, revised from the original for this book. Written about Catherine Gwatkin, later to be his wife, who he had met in about October, 1905.

December 31st (page 164)

A poem of two stanzas, 8 lines; probably written pre-1905. No details are known.

Hope And Despair (page 165)

A poem of two stanzas, 11 lines. Planned to be written on November 22, 1907, but was probably not written until the beginning of December, 1907. Although sent to the *Nation* in December, it was not published there until after publication in this book, q.v. (**549**).

Roses Can Wound (page 166)

A poem of two stanzas, 12 lines. It is not known when this was written, but probably pre-1905. No details are known. Although quotation marks appeared round the title in the contents list, they were omitted on the actual poem.

A Fear (page 167)

A poem of two stanzas, 14 lines. Originally published in the *Trawl*, q.v. (**612**) as one stanza under the title 'The Fear'. Revised for inclusion in this book.

Indignation: An Ode (page 168)

A poem, subdivided into four numbered parts, of 162 lines. He

From Lascelles to his Other Mother.

MARY AND THE BRAMBLE

BY

LASCELLES ABERCROMBIE

PUBLISHED BY THE AUTHOR
MUCH MARCLE
HEREFORDSHIRE
1910

Title page of *Mary and the Bramble* (item 3).

"THE SALE OF SAINT THOMAS,"

AN INTERLUDE,

BY

LASCELLES ABERCROMBIE,

Will be published immediately by the Author; price of each copy, including postage, THIRTEEN PENCE.

(Mr. Abercrombie will be extremely obliged if this announcement be communicated to persons likely to be interested in the matter.)

Pre-publication notice for *The Sale of St Thomas*, 1911 (item 4).

started writing it on November 21, 1907, completing the first two stanzas the following day. However, he did not finish the preliminary writing until about December 6, 1907; it still required 'polishing' by December 17.

The publication of 'Blind' in the *Independent Review* was the first step to L. A.'s decision to compile a volume of poetry, as he says in a letter of January 11, 1907: '. . . we must not miss the opportunity this publication of Blind may bring. For – in your ear – I see dimly possibilities of a volume arising out of that.' He had written relatively little poetry at that time, but his head was crammed with ideas, and he got to work to put them on paper. Five months later the book had been thoroughly planned. In a letter of June 19, 1907, he puts the idea forward: 'I purpose to make up the volume as follows:—

1. The New God
2. Blind
3. An Escape
Still making { 4. Vashti
5. A Dream Out Of Wales
6. The Fool's Adventure

What shall I call it? "Six Interludes". "Six Chamber Plays".'

A little optimistic perhaps as he had not yet found a publisher, although he had John Lane in mind; it had been Lane who had originally published 'Blind'. The continual refusal given to his poems by periodicals slightly depressed him, and on August 14, he said: 'I expect there will be considerable difficulty in inducing a publisher to take on the volume'. But on September 1 he decided to send 'The Miracle', 'The Escape', and 'The Fool's Adventure' to John Lane for consideration.

Goldsworthy Lowes Dickinson, a reader for the *Nation* and a scholar at Cambridge, had been extremely impressed with L. A.'s work, and he had been one of the people who had helped to get 'Blind' into the *Independent Review*.* He again used his influence with Lane, and wrote on November 19 urging him to bring the book out. Still L. A. was uncertain, '. . . if Lane does undertake to publish the book, he will pay me hardly anything or nothing and I shall be lucky if I don't have to pay him. But that I won't do, come what may,' he said on November 20. But the following day he received a letter from Lane that dispelled those worries. The terms of publication were that he was to receive 10 per cent royalty after 1,000 copies had been sold. He was extremely pleased, but Lane went on to say that he had not got enough 'copy'. As L. A. had nothing else completed he got to work imme-

* Catherine Gwatkin, L. A.'s fiancée, was a great friend of Christabelle Iles who was engaged to Hugh Meredith. He was at Cambridge University with G. Lowes Dickinson who had considerable influence in the publishing 'world', and who sent it to the editor of the *Independent Review*.

diately on the poems he had in skeleton form, advising Lane by the next post that he accepted the terms. (Even so, Dickinson advised him that although he shouldn't get better terms for a first book of poetry, he should refuse Lane's offer, trying periodicals with all the poems, and when they were all published in periodicals, try another publisher with the book.)

He was given until the second or third week in December to get the remaining work to Lane; therefore Vashti, which he would not have been able to finish in time ('Vashti . . . is a disappointment, as in some ways I think it the best I have done. However, perhaps that is for the best, as now I shall be able to get on leisurely at it and make it as big as I want it to be; hurry might have made me scamp the last scene, and that would have spoilt it all,'* he said on November 22) and 'A Dream Out of Wales' (a dramatic poem of which, unless the name has been changed, there is no trace) were dropped.

He did not really want to include a miscellaneous section of poems, but found it was necessary as there was not enough material for the book. He collected the poems he had written before he had thought of the volume being published, and the poems he had published in the *Nation*. All the final material was sent to Lane on December 19, 1907.

The dedication was decided upon on November 26, and the title on December 12. L. A. went to London in January, 1908 to clear up any remaining queries before the book was published. 384 copies had been sold in Britain, and 50 in America by June 30, 1908.

(2) INTERLUDES AND POEMS

Second edition:

1928 INTERLUDES AND | POEMS | *by* | LASCELLES ABERCROMBIE | JOHN LANE | THE BODLEY HEAD LTD

Format: Foolscap 8vo, $6\frac{3}{4} \times 4\frac{3}{8}$ ins.

Collation: viii + 216 pages, consisting of:—
half-title and imprint [*The Week-End Library*], verso blank (pp. i–ii); title page in ornamental border, imprint and details of publication on verso (pp. iii–iv); dedication [*To Catherine*], acknowledgements and note on verso (pp. v–vi); *Contents*, verso blank (pp. vii–viii); fly-title [*The New God: A Miracle*], verso blank (pp. 1–2); pages 3–213, text; page 214 blank; advertisements (pp. 215–216).

Binding: (i) red cloth; gilt lettering and ornament on spine; gilt facsimile of autograph, and blind impression of ornamental border on front cover; white end papers; top of leaves dyed red; all edges cut.

★ Vashti was later included in *Emblems of Love*, q.v. (5).

18

(ii) [second binding state, *c.* 1942] green cloth; gilt lettering on spine; gilt facsimile of autograph on front cover; white end papers; all edges cut.

Signatures: A^{16} B–G^{16}.

Publication Date: April 20, 1928 [3s. 6d.]

Contents: as the first edition (1908), except:—

Ceremonial Ode (Intended For A University)

This has been revised, and is now dedicated for the Jubilee of the University of Leeds, 1925.

'Roses Can Wound'

Quotation marks have been added to the title of the poem.

The Fear

The name has been changed from 'A Fear', and has again been revised for this edition.

(3) MARY AND THE BRAMBLE

First edition:

1910 MARY AND THE BRAMBLE | BY | LASCELLES ABERCROMBIE | PUBLISHED BY THE AUTHOR | MUCH MARCLE | HEREFORDSHIRE | 1910

Format: Crown 8vo, $7\frac{1}{4} \times 4\frac{3}{4}$ ins.

Collation: 12 unnumbered pages, consisting of:—
title page, verso blank (pp. 1–2); dedication [*To My Mother*], verso blank (pp. 3–4); pages 5–12, text.

Binding: blue card wrapper; black lettering on front cover; imprint on outside back cover; no end papers; all edges cut.

Signatures: None (one gathering).

Publication Date: (mid-) September, 1910 [1s.].

A poem of 182 lines; he began writing it just before May 6, 1908, finishing, after much revision and cutting, on September 19, 1908.

In 1910 it was refused publication in both the *Nation* and the *English Review.* He said in a letter of May 25, 1910: 'If I can't get it printed in a magazine (and I don't expect I shall be able to do so) I am going to publish it myself.' By August 5 he had definitely decided to publish it himself – 'suitable for Christmas cards.' A pre-publication leaflet was distributed (no trace has been found of the actual wording), and the booklet sold very well. By October 2, the first impression of 300 copies had sold out (at a net profit of about £9), and an immediate order was placed with the printers for a second impression; an uncertain number were printed, probably either 200 or 300. This was ready in mid-October, 1910 (with the title page: MARY AND THE BRAMBLE | BY | LASCELLES ABERCROMBIE | *SECOND IMPRESSION* | PUBLISHED BY THE AUTHOR | MUCH MARCLE | HEREFORDSHIRE | 1910).

Later published as part of *Twelve Idyls and Other Poems*, q.v. (**28**), and in the section *Twelve Idyls* in *Poems*, q.v. (**30**).

(4)   THE SALE OF SAINT THOMAS   [Act I]

First edition:

1911   THE | SALE OF SAINT THOMAS | BY | LASCELLES ABERCROMBIE | PUBLISHED BY THE AUTHOR | RYTON, DYMOCK | GLOUCESTERSHIRE | 1911

Format: Crown 8vo, $7\frac{1}{4} \times 4\frac{3}{4}$ ins.

Collation: 32 pages, consisting of:—
title page, verso blank (pp. 1–2); dedication [*To Arthur Ransome My Friend*], *The Tradition* on verso (pp. 3–4); pages 5–29, text; page 30 blank; advertisement for *Mary And The Bramble*, verso blank (pp. 31–32).

Binding: blue card wrapper; black lettering on front cover; imprint on outside back cover; no end papers; all edges cut.

Signatures: None (one gathering).

Publication Date: August (8?), 1911 [1s.].
A dramatic poem of 555 lines. Uncertain when it was written; probably 1909 to 1910 (it was certainly finished by the beginning of 1911).

Very few details are known about the publication arrangements of this, but on June 30, 1911 he said, 'I am bringing out St. Thomas soon; same style as Mary. The expenses will be slightly heavier, but I am determined to go on publishing my own things unless they actually bankrupt me.' A pre-publication notice was distributed, saying: '"THE SALE OF SAINT THOMAS", AN INTERLUDE, BY LASCELLES ABERCROMBIE, Will be published immediately by the Author; price of each copy, including postage, THIRTEEN PENCE. (Mr. Abercrombie will be extremely obliged if this announcement be communicated to persons likely to be interested in the matter.)' A subscription form was attached. Probably 500 copies were printed; it did not sell as well as *Mary And The Bramble*.

Later included in *Georgian Poetry, 1911–1912*, q.v. (**101**), and *Poems*, q.v. (**30**); also as act I of the completed six acts in 1930, q.v. (**31**).

(5)   EMBLEMS OF LOVE

First edition:

1911 EMBLEMS OF LOVE | DESIGNED IN SEVERAL [1912] DISCOURSES | BY LASCELLES ABERCROMBIE | *"Wonder it is to see in diverse mindes | How diversly love doth his pageaunts play"* | *"Ego tamquam centrum circuli, cui simili modo | se habent circumferentiæ partes"* | LONDON: JOHN LANE, THE BODLEY HEAD | NEW YORK: JOHN LANE COMPANY. MCMXII

Format: Crown 8vo, $7\frac{3}{8} \times 4\frac{7}{8}$ ins.

Collation: viii + 216 pages, consisting of:—
half-title, note [*By the same Author*] on verso (pp. i–ii); title page, imprint on verso (pp. iii–iv); dedication [*To My Wife*], verso blank (pp. v–vi); contents [*Table*], verso blank (pp. vii–viii); fly-title [*Emblems of Love*], verso blank (pp. 1–2); pages 3–213, text; page 214, acknowledgements; advertisement (pp. 215–216).

Binding: (i) green cloth; gilt lettering and ornament on spine and front cover; white end papers; top edges of leaves gilt; fore and lower edges uncut. (ii) [second binding state probably of a slightly later date] green cloth (paler than (i)); gilt lettering and ornament on spine ('The Bodley Head' on spine is more condensed than in (i)); red lettering and ornament on front cover; white end papers; top of leaves dyed green; fore and lower edges uncut. [Some copies of the second state appear to have had the gilt omitted from the lettering and ornament on the spine.]

Signatures: A^4 B–O^8 P^4.

Publication Date: December 12, 1911 [5s.].

Contents: 'Table'.

Hymn To Love (page 3).

> A poem of ten stanzas, 40 lines. It was probably written in July, 1910, being refused publication in the *Nation* in August, 1910. Later accepted by the *Vineyard*, q.v. (**616**).

Prelude (page 7)

A dramatic poem of 234 lines; possibly started on June 24, 1908. Finished July to August, 1908.

Vashti (page 16)

A dramatic poem of five acts, with the number of lines: Act I, 228; II, 433; III, 595; IV, 299 (subdivided into four parts: 1, 120 lines; 2, 52; 3, 45; 4, 82). The acts are entitled: I, Ahasuerus and Vashti; II, The Feast of Kings: Midnight; III, Vashti and the King's Women at their Feast; IV, 1, no title; 2, The First Vision, Helen; 3, The Second Vision, Sappho; 4, The Third Vision, Theresa.

It is not known when he began writing this, but it was probably mid-1906. Apparently he scrapped his first attempt *c.* June, 1907, and started again, finishing the first act on August 17, 1907. He was disappointed when he found he was unable to finish it in time for *Interludes and Poems* (see the notes of that book), and in fact it took him until about June, 1908, before it was completed.

IMPERFECTION

Three Girls In Love:

Mary: A Legend of the '45 (page 77)

A dramatic poem of six acts, with the titles and number of lines: Act I (A street in Carlisle leading to the Scottish gate), 65; II (The Scottish gate, Carlisle), 55; III (Mary lying awake in bed), 89; IV (At dawn. The Scottish gate), 35; V (Katerina and Jean), 69; VI (Before dawn. At the Scottish gate), 64.

He began writing this on June 24, 1908, and by July 6 was working on the fourth act. By August 10 he had finished and sent it to the *New Quarterly*, but it was refused; on August 15 he began to revise it. It was probably finally finished at the end of September, 1908. Originally it had been entitled 'The Forty Five'.

Jean (page 95)

A dramatic poem of four acts, with the titles and number of lines: Act I (The parlour of a public house), 125; II (Jean by herself, undressing), 24; III (Morris by himself), 27; IV (The public house), 100.

Very little is known about this poem, but it was probably written 1909 to 1910.

Katrina (page 109)

A dramatic poem of two acts, with the titles and number of lines: Act I (On the sea coast), 214; II (In Sylvan's house), 82.

This poem was probably written in 1909 or 1910.

Judith (page 127)

A dramatic poem of four acts, with the titles and number of lines: Act I (The besieged city of Bethulia), 598; II (Before the tent of Holofernes), 81; III (In the tent of Holofernes), 195; IV (At the gate of Bethulia), 674.

He had planned, but not started, this by July 12, 1907; it was not written until c. 1910–11.

The Eternal Wedding (page 188)

A dramatic poem of 314 lines. Planned but not started by August 10, 1908; probably started c. October 18, 1908: 'I decided . . . to put it in a form unusual for such enterprises; namely . . . a converse between "He" and "She". So that it will be something of a complement to Vashti.' It is uncertain when it was finished, but probably around February, 1909.

Marriage Song (page 200)

A poem subdivided into four parts, with the number of lines: Part I, 57; II, 40; III, 49; IV, 21. He probably began writing this in October, 1908, intending to finish it by January 23, 1909, his wedding day. In fact, it was not finished until c. February or March, 1909, if not later.

Epilogue (: Dedication) (page 209)

A poem of 146 lines. This was written as a birthday poem for his fiancée, Catherine Gwatkin. Although the birthday in question was April 13, 1908, he did not write it until August or September of that year. The original length was 330 lines, which was revised and reduced for inclusion in this book.

On July 5, 1908, he wrote, 'An idea has occurred to me lately to make a book of interludes . . . all dealing from various points of view with Love, and making up when all put together a kind of Treatise of Love'. He took the morning off from the *Liverpool Courier* on August 10 to work out the details, and he outlined them in a letter: 'The scheme, which is of course not wholly filled up as yet, consists of three parts. Part 1. Love Ripening. Part 2. Love Ripe and Overripe. Part 3. Seed of Love. The first part deals with the progress of sensual, selfish imperfect love, as it must have begun, to the perfect reciprocal love. . . . The second part consists of instances of how love works on different natures, and some of love's over-growths and mis-shapen growths. . . . The third part is kind of mystical, and deals with Love as the type of Eternity. . . .'

He decided 'Vashti' for part 1, and 'Mary: A Legend of the '45' for part 2, but had not considered a place for any of the other poems he had written. However, on September 19, 1908, he began to gather them together. By June 30, 1911, the book was ready for publication, the name now set at *Emblems of Love*, but he had not secured a publisher, although naturally he had considered Lane. It is not known when Lane accepted the book, but by November 22, 1911, L. A. had corrected the proofs, and was expecting it to be published in early December.

Published in the U.S.A. July (20?), 1912.

(6)   THOMAS HARDY

First edition:

1912   THOMAS HARDY | A CRITICAL STUDY | BY | LASCELLES ABERCROMBIE | LONDON | MARTIN SECKER | NUMBER FIVE JOHN STREET | ADELPHI | MCMXII

Format: Demy 8vo, $8\frac{3}{4} \times 5\frac{5}{8}$ ins.

Collation: 226 pages, consisting of:—
half-title, note [*uniform with this volume*] on verso (pp. 1–2); recto blank, photograph (of Thomas Hardy, by H. W. Barnett, with tissue protection) on verso (pp. 3–4); title page, verso blank (pp. 5–6); *Note*, signed by L. A. (pp. 7–8); *Contents*, verso blank (pp. 9–10); pages 11–225, text; imprint on page 225; page 226 blank.

Binding: dark blue cloth; gilt lettering on spine; gilt lettering and ornament in double line border on front cover; white end papers; top edges of leaves gilt; fore and lower edges uncut.

Signatures: π^8 (–π7) A^2 (–A2) B–O^8 P^2 (–P2).

Publication Date: October, 1912 [7s. 6d.].

Contents:

> Introductory
> Characteristics
> Minor Novels
> Annexes
> Dramatic Form
> Epic Form
> The Poems
> The Dynasts

L. A. has always been a great admirer of Thomas Hardy, as he says in a letter of February 10, 1910, immediately after reading *Tess of the D'Urbevilles*: 'Hardy has made the novel do the work of drama and the epic: there is none like him, none'. He approached Martin Secker in about November, 1911, asking if he might contribute a book to a series of critical studies Secker had been running. Secker consented, and on about March 10, 1912, he started writing, finishing chapter I (Introductory) on March 15. Probably in mid-1912 L. A. went to see Hardy, and in an undated letter he described the meeting: 'I had a most disastrous interview with Hardy. I think he really is a dear old man, but evidently worried by interviews. At any rate he was not in the least placated by a very polite and deferential note I sent him, but on the contrary was annoyed I should call on him at all, and especially annoyed that I should call on him about his own work. He refused to say anything – if I chose to write a study it was nothing to him and did not interest him; and it should be done merely from the books, he himself would not give any assistance. And so on. I believe he thought me about 19 years old. When I promised not to print anything he might say, "O they all say that, and then do it". With that he bowed me out.'

By September 3, 1912, he had completed the book and it had been sent to the publishers. Later that month he went to London from Dymock, Gloucestershire, to correct the proofs, finishing there on September 27.

1,000 copies were printed. A second binding state of the first impression was issued slightly later, or perhaps at the same time, with sixteen pages of advertisements added to the end, headed 'Autumn Books . . . September MCMXII'. In about October, 1913, a second impression was issued, bound in black cloth, with the advertisements headed 'Autumn Books MCMXIII . . .' In 1915 a third impression was issued in black cloth with the advertisements amended again. It was distributed in the U.S.A. by Mitchell Kennerley, published in 1913.

This book was the turning point in L. A.'s change over from Lane to Secker as his publisher. Although the terms of his first book (*Interludes and Poems*) had pleased him very much, L. A. became more displeased as the arrangements for his other books were going on, and the impersonal attitude taken by Lane did not increase L. A.'s confidence. When he brought out his two booklets published by himself (*Mary and the Bramble*, and *The Sale of Saint Thomas*), it is probable both John Lane and Martin Secker received copies. John Lane was probably not very pleased, but when L. A. turned to Secker (a natural turn, as Secker was a young up-and-coming publisher to whom many writers were attracted) and offered to write *Thomas Hardy*, getting it published before *Deborah*, this was the last straw as far as Lane was concerned. *Deborah*, that had almost certainly been in Lane's hands for some time before it actually appeared, was finished off and published two months after *Thomas Hardy*; L. A. made that book his last dealing with Lane, and from then until 1931 he dealt almost exclusively with Secker [see the notes on *The Sale of Saint Thomas* (**31**)].

25

First edition: second (American) impression:

1912 THOMAS HARDY | A CRITICAL STUDY | BY |
[1964] LASCELLES ABERCROMBIE | *New York* | RUSSELL
& RUSSELL | 1964

Format: Demy 8vo, $8\frac{5}{8} \times 5\frac{3}{4}$ ins.

Collation: 224 pages (numbered 3–226), consisting of:—
half-title, photograph (of Thomas Hardy, by H. W. Barnett) on verso
(pp. 1–2); title page, note on publication and imprint on verso (pp.
3–4); *Note*, signed by L. A. (pp. 5–6); *Contents*, verso blank (pp. 7–8);
pages 9–223, text; page 224 blank.

Binding: green cloth; gilt lettering on spine; white end papers; fore and
lower edges uncut.

Signatures: Unsigned: $1-7^{16}$.

Issued: December, 1964 [$6.50].

Contents: as the first impression.

'It is not possible . . . to give . . . the exact number printed: our books
are printed in small quantities, but frequently reprinted.'

Pages 1–2 were excluded in this photo-offset reprint in order that
the note on page 2 of the original might be omitted without changing
the page numbering.

Second edition:

1919 THOMAS HARDY | A CRITICAL STUDY | BY |
LASCELLES ABERCROMBIE | LONDON | MAR-
TIN SECKER | XVII BUCKINGHAM STREET |
ADELPHI

Format: Pott 8vo, $6\frac{5}{8} \times 4\frac{1}{4}$ ins.

Collation: 176 pages, consisting of:—
half-title, details of publication on verso (pp. 1–2); title page, imprint
on verso (pp. 3–4); *Note*, signed by L. A. (pp. 5–6); *Contents*, verso
blank (pp. 7–8); pages 9–176, text; imprint on page 176.

Binding: green boards; white paper label on spine, with orange
lettering; white end papers; fore and lower edges uncut.

Signatures: A^8 B–L^8.

Publication Date: 1919 [3s. 6d.]

Contents: as the first edition (1912).
1,000 copies were printed.

(9)   THOMAS HARDY

Third edition:

1924   Thomas Hardy | A Critical Study | By Lascelles Abercrombie | London: Martin Secker | Number Five John Street | Adelphi mcmxxiv

Format: Demy 8vo, $7\frac{1}{2} \times 5\frac{1}{2}$ ins.

Collation: 200 pages, consisting of:—

half-title, note [*By the same Author*] on verso (pp. 1–2); title page, imprint and note [*Bibliography*] on verso (pp. 3–4); *Contents*, verso blank (pp. 5–6); pages 7–196, text; imprint on page 196; advertisements (pp. 197–200).

Binding: buff boards; yellow cloth spine; black lettering on spine; white end papers; top of leaves dyed black; fore and lower edges uncut.

Signatures: A^8 B–M^8 N^4.

Publication Date: 1924 [6s.].

Contents: as the first edition (1912).

1,000 copies were printed. In 1927 a second impression of 1,000 copies was printed with the title page: Thomas Hardy | A Critical Study | By Lascelles Abercrombie | *FOURTH PRINTING* | London: Martin Secker | Number Five John Street | Adelphi mcmxxvii. Two more leaves were added, the advertisements now covering pages 197–202, pages 203–204 blank (the signatures being A^8 B–M^8 N^6). A third impression of 1,000 copies was printed in 1935 with the title page: Thomas Hardy | A Critical Study | By Lascelles Abercrombie | *FIFTH PRINTING* | London: Martin Secker | Number Five John Street | Adelphi mcmxxxv. The advertisements were omitted completely, the signatures now being A^8 B–L^8 M^{10}.

In 1927 an impression was distributed in the U.S.A. by the Viking Press of New York.

First edition:

1912   DEBORAH | A PLAY IN THREE ACTS | BY LAS-
[1913] CELLES ABERCROMBIE | LONDON: JOHN LANE
THE BODLEY HEAD | NEW YORK: JOHN LANE
COMPANY | TORONTO: BELL & COCKBURN
MCMXIII

Format: Crown 8vo, $7\frac{5}{8} \times 4\frac{3}{4}$ ins.

Collation: viii+64 pages, consisting of:—
blank leaf (pp. i–ii); half-title, verso blank (pp. iii–iv); title page,
imprint on verso (pp. v–vi); dedication [*To Patrick Abercrombie*], verso
blank (pp. vii–viii); fly-title [*Act I*], *Persons* on verso (pp. 1–2); pages
3–60, text; note [*The acting rights are the exclusive property of the Author.*],
verso blank (pp. 61–62); advertisements (pp. 63–64).

Binding: dove-grey boards; green cloth spine; white paper labels on
spine and front cover, with black lettering; white end papers; all edges
uncut; two spare labels tipped in between page 64 and end paper.

Signatures: π^4 A–D^8

Publication Date: December 13, 1912 [1s. 6d.].

Deborah, a poetic drama in three acts with the number of lines:
Act I, 555; II, 522; III, 436, was first planned in October, 1908. By
December, 1909, he had written the first act as a play on its own
calling it 'The Sick Land'. He went to London in October, 1910, to
try and get it staged. There he read it to Miss Gertrude Kingston –
'She liked "The Sick Land" best of all the plays; it held her, she said,
and it moved her. And she thought seriously of finding a place for
it in a future programme. But she did not at all like the notion of
prolonging the story into three acts. . . . So I told her that my notion . . .
was not so much to produce a Three Act Play as a Trilogy of Three
One Act plays, each complete in itself . . .'. He set to work almost
immediately on the other two acts, and by the end of January, 1911,
they were completed, except for some minor alterations. Act II he
titled 'The Power of Life', and Act III, 'The Gabriel Hounds'. It was
not staged by Miss Kingston, or by a Madame Strindberg who was
arranging for it to be staged in September, 1912, for the opening of
a theatre or club in London on October 15, 1912. The only production
(of one performance only) was by the Theatre Players, Oxford;
produced by Joy Masefield at Josca's Little Theatre, Oxford, on April
27, 1964 (a production of the first act only).

Cast:

> Saul: Steven Meeson
> Deborah: Wendy Caws
> Mother: Jennifer Stephens
> Martin: Ken Brampton
> A Doctor: Jack Foster

Supported by Jacky Cockburn, Irene Good, Ruth Harris, Maria Krieger, Judy Lane, Jean Wood, John Aveyard, Bob Coats, and Brian Kinch.

(11)   DEBORAH

Second edition:

1923 DEBORAH | A PLAY IN THREE ACTS | BY LAS-CELLES ABERCROMBIE | LONDON | JOHN LANE THE BODLEY HEAD LIMITED

Format: Crown 8vo, $7\frac{3}{8} \times 5\frac{7}{8}$ ins.

Collation: 76 pages, consisting of:—
half title, note [*By the same Author*] in single line border and panels on verso (pp. 1–2); title page, imprint and details of publication on verso (pp. 3–4); dedication [*To Patrick Abercrombie*], verso blank (pp. 5–6); fly-title [*Act I*], *Persons* on verso (pp. 7–8); pages 9–71, text; page 72 blank; note [*The acting rights are the exclusive property of the Author*], verso blank (pp. 73–74); advertisements (pp. 75–76).

Binding: green cloth; gilt lettering on spine; white end papers; top of leaves dyed green; fore and lower edges uncut.

Signatures: A^8 B–D^8 E^6.

Publication Date: April 27, 1923.

The text of the play has been slightly revised, but is the same number of lines. It was planned for reissue in 1922 (the first proofs being dated April 29, 1922).

(12)   SPECULATIVE DIALOGUES

First edition:

1913 SPECULATIVE DIALOGUES | BY LASCELLES ABERCROMBIE | [ornament] | LONDON: MARTIN SECKER | NUMBER FIVE JOHN STREET ADELPHI

Format: Crown 8vo, $7\frac{3}{8} \times 4\frac{7}{8}$ ins.

Collation: 208 pages, consisting of:—
half-title, note [*By the same Author*] on verso (pp. 1–2); title page, note on publication on verso (pp. 3–4); quotation [*È un principe-sacerdote tra loro che s'appella 'Hoh', et in lingua nostra si dice 'Metafisico'. Questo è capo di tutti in spirituale et in temporale, et tutti li negozî in lui si terminano. – La Città del Sole.*], verso blank (pp. 5–6); *Contents,* verso blank (pp. 7–8); fly-title [*I | Famine And Pestilence*], verso blank (pp. 9–10); pages 11–203, text; imprint on page 204; advertisements (pp. 205–208).

Binding: (i) green cloth; black lettering on white label on spine; white end papers; fore and lower edges uncut. (ii) brown cloth; black lettering on white paper label on spine; white end papers; top of leaves dyed brown; fore and lower edges uncut. (iii) pink Michelet paper boards; brown lettering on white paper label on spine; white end papers; fore and lower edges uncut. (iv) [fourth binding state by 'The Bomb Shop', *c.* 1919] red card; black lettering on spine, front and outside back covers; double line border and panels on front cover; no end papers; lower edges uncut.

Signatures: A^8 B–N^8.

Publication Date: October 23, 1913 [5s.].

Contents:

Famine and Pestilence (page 11)

> Probably written *c.* 1901–02, originally appearing in the *Trawl*, q.v. (**612**). It was completely revised and recast between September, 1907, and February 20, 1908. L. A. sent it to the *Albany Review* where it was later published, q.v. (**203**), being reprinted in *Littell's Living Age*, q.v. (**259**). Again revised before inclusion in this book.

Minos and a Ghost (page 33)

> No details are known of this, but it was possibly written in 1905, or earlier.

A Beggar and His Dog (On the Other Side of Death) (page 47)

> This was definitely written pre-December, 1905; probably in 1905.

Earth and a Crowd (page 71)
Lust and Love (Scene: The Mind of a Man in Sleep) (page 85)
Science and the World (page 115)
Philosophy and the Angel (page 159)
Time and Eternity (page 193)

> The five above were written between October, 1911 and about July, 1913 (see the notes below).

Upon completion of 'Famine and Pestilence', he wrote in a letter of February 20, 1908, 'If I remain satisfied (more or less) with this dialogue, I shall perhaps try some more, for it is a form of prose-writing I have always rather liked: I wrote dozens of dialogues in my youth . . .'. Certainly 'Famine and Pestilence', and possibly 'Minos and a Ghost', were from these dozens, but it was not until June, 1911, when he considered the idea again and saw Secker with a view to getting them published, that he wrote any more. It was to have been ready for publication in the Spring of 1912, but the large amount of work required to get *Emblems of Love* finished, coupled with the work he was doing on *Thomas Hardy*, delayed his chances of writing until about October, 1911. Eventually he got down to it, and it was finished and sent to the publishers on July 11, 1913.

Distributed in the U.S.A. by Mitchell Kennerley, published in 1913.

(13) POETRY AND CONTEMPORARY SPEECH

First edition:

1914 THE ENGLISH ASSOCIATION | Pamphlet No. 27 | Poetry and Contemporary Speech | By | Lascelles Abercrombie | February, 1914

Format: Royal 8vo, 9¾ × 6 ins.

Collation: 12 pages, consisting of:—
title page, verso blank (pp. 1–2); pages 3–12, text.

Binding: grey paper wrapper; black lettering on front cover; note on inside front cover; advertisements on inside and outside back cover; no end papers; all edges cut.

Signatures: None (one gathering).

Publication Date: February, 1914 [1s.].

This was a lecture as delivered to the English Association on January 9, 1914, at University College, London. Pages 10–12 of this were revised and expanded, to be published as pages 139–146 of the *Theory of Poetry*, q.v. (**22**).

(14) THE EPIC

First edition:

[1914] THE ART AND CRAFT OF LETTERS | THE EPIC | BY | LASCELLES | ABERCROMBIE | LONDON: MARTIN SECKER | NUMBER FIVE JOHN STREET ADELPHI

Format: Foolscap 8vo, 6¾ × 4¼ ins.

31

Collation: 96 pages, consisting of:—
half-titles and publisher's emblem, note [*Uniform with this volume*] on verso (pp. 1–2); title page in single line border and panels, verso blank (pp. 3–4); *Preface* (pp. 5–6); pages 7–96, text; imprint on page 96.

Binding: (i) black cloth; white paper label with red lettering on spine; white end papers; fore and lower edges uncut. [Some copies, possibly a variant binding, have all edges cut.] (ii) grey paper wrappers; black lettering on front cover in single line border and panels; black lettering on spine; no end papers; advertisements for the 'Art and Craft of Letters' series on outside back cover; fore and lower edges uncut.

Signatures: A^8 B–F^8.

Publication Date: May, 1914 (edition undated) [1s.].

This was written as 'an essay to consider epic poetry as a species of literature'. Distributed in the U.S.A. by H. Doran Co. of New York, probably published at a slightly later date.

(15) THE EPIC

First edition: second issue (combined binding)

[1914] THE ART AND CRAFT OF LETTERS | THE EPIC | BY | LASCELLES | ABERCROMBIE | LONDON: MARTIN SECKER | NUMBER FIVE JOHN STREET ADELPHI

Format: Foolscap 8vo, $6\frac{3}{4} \times 4\frac{1}{4}$ ins.

Collation: 224 pages, consisting of:—
half-titles and publisher's emblem, note [*Uniform with this volume*] on verso (pp. 1–2); title page (as above) in single line border and panels, verso blank (pp. 3–4); *Preface* (pp. 5–6); pages 7–96, text; imprint on page 96; blank leaf (pp. [97–98] 1–2); half-titles [of *The Short Story*], note [*Uniform with this volume*] on verso (pp. [99–100] 3–4); title page of *The Short Story*, verso blank (pp. [101–102] 5–6); pages [103–159] 7–63, text; imprint on page [160] 64; half-title [of *History*], note [*Uniform with this volume*] on verso (pp. [161–162] 1–2); title page of *History*, verso blank (pp. [163–164] 3–4); pages [165–222] 5–62, text; imprint, verso blank (pp. [223–224] 63–64).

Binding: grey boards; white cloth spine; black lettering in single line border on front cover; black lettering in double line red border on white label on spine; white end papers; all edges uncut.

Signatures: (of *The Epic* only) A^8 B–F^8.

Issue Date: It is not known for certain, but this is probably the remaining pages of the first impression issued *c.* 1931–32.

Variant bindings of *Lyrics and Unfinished Poems* (item 40).

VISION AND LOVE

LASCELLES ABERCROMBIE

LONDON:
ARts Research

Title page of *Vision and Love* (item 43).

Second edition:

1923   The Epic: an Essay | By Lascelles Abercrombie | London:
[1922] Martin Secker | Number Five John Street | Adelphi
       mcmxxii

> *Format:* Crown 8vo, $7\frac{1}{2} \times 5\frac{1}{2}$ ins.
>
> *Collation:* 128 pages, consisting of:—
> half-title, note [*By the same Author*] on verso (pp. 1–2); title page,
> imprint and details of publication on verso (pp. 3–4); *Preface* (pp. 5–6);
> pages 7–123, text; imprint on page 124; advertisements (pp. 125–128).
>
> *Binding:* buff boards; yellow cloth spine; black lettering on spine;
> white end papers; top of leaves dyed black; fore and lower edges
> uncut.
>
> *Signatures:* A^8 B–H^8.
>
> *Publication Date:* January, 1923 [5s.].

(17) AN ESSAY TOWARDS A THEORY OF ART

First edition:

1922   An Essay towards | a Theory of Art | By Lascelles Aber-
       crombie | London: Martin Secker | Number Five John
       Street | Adelphi mcmxxii

> *Format:* Crown 8vo, $7\frac{1}{2} \times 5\frac{1}{2}$ ins.
>
> *Collation:* 120 pages, consisting of:—
> half-title, note [*By the same Author*] on verso (pp. 1–2); title page, imprint
> on verso (pp. 3–4); *Table of the Argument* (pp. 5–7); ΦΙΛΑΛΗΘΕΣΙΝ
> on page 8; pages 9–115, text; imprint on page 116; advertisements
> (pp. 117–120).
>
> *Binding:* buff boards; yellow cloth spine; black lettering on spine;
> white end papers; top of leaves dyed black; fore and lower edges
> uncut.
>
> *Signatures:* A^8 B–G^8 H^4.
>
> *Publication Date:* May, 1922 [5s.].

   This was possibly based on a lecture given to the Newcastle Literary
and Philosophical Society, Newcastle, on December 19, 1921, probably written in the summer of 1920.

1,000 copies were printed of the first impression, and 1,000 copies of the second impression (issued in January, 1926) were printed with the title page: An Essay towards | a Theory of Art | By Lascelles Abercrombie | *SECOND IMPRESSION* | London: Martin Secker | Number Five John Street | Adelphi mcmxxvi.

(18)   FOUR SHORT PLAYS

First edition:

1922   Four Short Plays | By Lascelles Abercrombie | London: Martin Secker | Number Five John Street | Adelphi 1922

Format: Crown 8vo, $7\frac{3}{8} \times 5\frac{1}{2}$ ins.

Collation: 176 pages, consisting of:—
half-title, note [*By the same Author*] on verso (pp. 1–2); title page, imprint on verso (pp. 3–4); dedication [*To Edward Marsh*], verso blank (pp. 5–6); *Contents, Note* on the plays on verso (pp. 7–8); fly-title [*The Adder*], verso blank (pp. 9–10); pages 11–176, text; imprint on page 176.

Binding: buff boards; yellow cloth spine; black lettering on spine; white end papers; top of leaves dyed black; fore and lower edges uncut.

Signatures: A^8 B–L^8.

Publication Date: June (27?), 1922 [6s.].

Contents:

The Adder (page 11)

A poetic drama of 696 lines, which he had planned but not started by August 8, 1907. He started writing on September 22 of the same year, finishing it in the rough on June 24, 1908. It was still not completely satisfactory by mid-October, 1908. Originally published in *Poetry and Drama*, q.v. (**576**), being slightly revised from 694 lines for inclusion here.

The performances are as follows:—

1. March 3 to 8, 1913: produced by Basil Dean at the Liverpool Repertory Theatre, Liverpool (with Margaret Morris and Her Dancing Children, and Gilbert Cannan's *Miles Dixon*).

Cast:

Seth:	Lawrence Hanray
Newby:	J. H. Roberts
The Squire:	Norman McKeown
The Girl:	Eileen Thorndike.

Note: there were seven performances in all.

2. May 17 to 23, 1913: produced by John Drinkwater at the Birmingham Repertory Theatre, Birmingham (with Lady Gregory's *The White Cockade*).

Cast:

Seth:	'John Darnley' [John Drinkwater]
Newby:	Ivor Barnard
The Squire:	Felix Aylmer
The Girl:	Cecily Byrne

Note: there were seven performances in all. It is not certain what parts Aylmer and Barnard played, but Aylmer was probably the Squire, and Barnard was probably Newby.

The Staircase (page 49)

A poetic drama of 606 lines, which he was in the middle of writing in August, 1913. Originally published in *New Numbers*, q.v. (**564**) as 601 lines, being slightly revised for inclusion in this book. It got second prize at the Three Arts Club, London, competition for one act plays in November, 1914. There may have been a performance for this competition, but no details are known.

The only definite known production was by Jackson Wilcox on March 4, 9, 11, and 16, 1920 (four special matinée performances only) at The Playhouse, Liverpool (with *The End of the World*).

Cast: unknown, except Clifford Marle was the joiner, and Rita John was the woman. The remaining four were taken from the following: John C. Bland, A. B. Douglass, J. Gordon Fleming, Leo Montgomery, G. Malcolm Russell, and Glynn Williams.

The Deserter (page 85)

A poetic drama of 674 lines which he finished writing on or just before November 6, 1921. It was published in *Theatre Arts Magazine*, q.v. (**594**) at about the same time as its inclusion in this book.

He considered making this the first act of a three act play.

It is alleged there was a performance at the Leeds Arts Theatre in the 1920's, but no mention of this can be found anywhere. The only definite performances known are:—

1. (probably early-) 1927: production of the Jewish Arts Society by an unknown producer, possibly in Birmingham.
   Cast: unknown.

   Note: probably one performance only. This was entered in the National Community Festival Competition arranged by the British Drama League.

2. October 30 to November 1, 1952: produced by a Mr. Erskine or Mr. Sayer at Malvern College, Worcestershire (with Anton Thekoff's *The Proposal*, and Richard B. Sheridan's *The Critic*).

Cast:

1st Woman:	A. D. Wright
2nd Woman:	J. R. de W. Harrison
1st Man:	D. P. R. Brass
2nd Man:	D. Smeeton
3rd Man:	D. Griffiths
Luther:	I. Hilton-Bailey
The Girl:	I. E. Jones
Martha:	P. St. G. Verriour
The Soldier:	S. Radcliffe

Note: there were three performances in all. This was probably an all male cast, the female parts being played by boy pupils of the college.

The End of the World (page 123)

A poetic drama of two acts, with the number o lines: Act I, was; II, 508. It is not known when he started writing this, but act I 507 completed in August, 1913. It was completely finished by the beginning of February, 1914, just before being sent to the printers for inclusion in *New Numbers*, q.v. (**562**), where it originally appeared [dedicated *To E. M.*]. An extract from *New Numbers* was included in *Poetry and Drama*, q.v. (**578**), and it was later published again in full in *Georgian Poetry, 1913–1915*, q.v. (**102**). It was slightly revised from act I, 508 lines, act II, 506, for inclusion here.

The performances are as follows:—

1. September 12 to 18, 1914: produced by John Drinkwater at the Birmingham Repertory Theatre, Birmingham (with Samuel Foote's *The Liar*).

   Cast: unknown who plays what part, but all the following are in it: Felix Aylmer, Ivor Barnard, John Drinkwater, John Dunn-Yarker, E. Stuart Vinden, W. Ribton Haines, and Noel Shammon; one of the following actresses played Mrs. Huff: Cecily Byrne, Margaret Chatwin, Margaret Dudley, Maud Gill, Cathleen Orford, Betty Pinchard, or Mary Raby.

   Note: there were seven performances in all.

2. October 26 to 31, 1914: production of the Bristol Playgoers Club by Muriel Pratt at the Theatre Royal, Bristol (with John Masefield's *Philip The King*).

   Cast:

Huff:	Brember Wills
Sollers:	Ernest Bodkin
Merrick:	not known
The Stranger:	Clive Carey
Vine:	B. Marsh Dunn

Shale:	not known
Mrs. Huff:	Susan Claughton
Warp:	J. Denton Thompson

Note: there were six performances in all.

3. March 4, 9, 11, 16, 1920: produced by Jackson Wilcox at the Playhouse, Liverpool (with *The Staircase*).

Cast:

Huff:	Andrew Money
Sollers:	Cliff Page
Merrick:	Stuart Lomath
The Stranger:	Deering Wells
Vine:	James Harecourt
Shale:	Richard Bird
Mrs. Huff:	Linda Gibbs
Warp:	Frederick Francis

Note: these were four special matinée performances only.

4. December 9, 10, 11, 1920: producer unknown, at the Little Theatre, Manchester (with Gordon Bottomley's *King Lear's Wife*).

Cast: unknown, except Amy Buxton Nowell played Mrs. Huff.

5. February 16, 1923: production of the Leeds University Choral and Dramatic Society by an unknown producer (with no other play).

Cast: not known.

Note: one performance only. The same production was to have been performed at the Industrial Theatre, Leeds, on February 19 and 20, 1923, but was cancelled because two of the cast fell ill.

6. October 14, 1932: produced by Cyril Wood on the British Broadcasting Corporation, Western Region station only, at 9.35 p.m. (with Nicholas Evreinov's *A Merry Death*).

Cast: not known.

7. January 16, 1933: there was probably a performance on this date, possibly in Sheffield, but no details can be found.

8. March 20 and 27, 1938: production of the Contemporary Theatre Club by Eve Acton-Bond at Finchley Road, London, N.W.8 (with Molière's *The Romantic Ladies*).

Cast:

Huff:	Brandon Acton-Bond
Sollers:	John Jameson
Merrick:	Patrick Ross
The Stranger:	Bruce Adams
Vine:	Philip Holles

Shale: Henry Rayner
Mrs. Huff: Julie Mars
Warp: Jonathan Field
supported by Diana Barry, Kenneth Gordon, and Denis Ryder.

Note: four performances in all. An overture was composed specially for this production by Barrett Preston.

By August 14, 1918, L. A. had planned this book, approaching Martin Secker later that year. After negotiations had been completed, he set to work to complete the last of the four plays – 'The Deserter' – and in mid-March, 1922, he sent the manuscript to the publisher. The proofs were corrected in April, 1922.

(19)   PRINCIPLES OF ENGLISH PROSODY

First edition:

1923   Principles of | English Prosody | By Lascelles Abercrombie | Part I | The Elements | London: Martin Secker | Number Five John Street | Adelphi mcmxxiii

Format: Crown 8vo, $7\frac{3}{8} \times 5\frac{1}{2}$ ins.

Collation: 160 pages, consisting of:—
blank leaf (pp. 1–2); half-title, note [*By the same Author*] on verso (pp. 3–4); title page, imprint on verso (pp. 5–6); *Preface* signed by L. A. (pp. 7–11); page 12 blank; pages 13–156, text; imprint on page 156; advertisements (pp. 157–160).

Binding: buff boards; yellow cloth spine; black lettering on spine; white end papers; top of leaves dyed black; fore and lower edges uncut.

Signatures: A^8 B–K^8.

Publication Date: May, 1923 [5s.].

Only Part I appeared; a second part, to be called 'systematic conspectus of versification', was planned, but was never written.
This was probably based on eight lectures given at the University of Leeds on January 10, 17, 24, 31, February 7, 14, 21, 28, 1922.
There was possibly a second impression of this issued in 1926, but no trace of a copy has been found.

First edition:

1923   Phoenix | Tragicomedy in Three Acts | By Lascelles
       Abercrombie | London: Martin Secker | Number Five
       John Street | Adelphi 1923

Format: Crown 8vo, $7\frac{3}{8} \times 5\frac{1}{2}$ ins.

Collation: 96 pages, consisting of:—
half-title, note [*By the same Author*] on verso (pp. 1–2); title page, ten
line Greek quotation from *Iliad IX* and imprint on verso (pp. 3–4);
dedication [*To John Drinkwater*], *Persons* etc. on verso (pp. 5–6);
pages 7–95, text; imprint on page 95; page 96 blank.

Binding: (i) buff boards; yellow cloth spine; black lettering on spine;
white end papers; top of leaves dyed black; fore and lower edges uncut.
(ii) [second binding state, *c.* 1932] yellow cloth; black lettering on
spine; white end papers; all edges cut.

Signatures: A^8 B–F^8.

Publication Date: September (15?), 1923 [5s.].

Phoenix, a poetic drama, is in three acts with the number of lines:
Act I, 689; II, 423; III, 604. He probably started writing this in early
August, 1918, finishing the first act in mid-September of the same
year. It is not known how long it took to finish the other acts, but the
complete manuscript was typed in October, 1922.
    The performances are as follows:—

1. January 20, 1924: produced by Basil Dean at St. Martin's Theatre,
   London (with Gordon Bottomley's *Gruach*).

       Cast:
           1st Soldier: Ian Hunter
           2nd Soldier: Austin Trevor
           The Queen: Barbara Gott
           Amyntor: Leslie Banks
           Rhodope: Mary Clare
           Phoenix: Robert Harris

    Note: one performance only, being the first Gala performance for
    the Playbox subscribers.

2. March 31 to April 5, 1924: production of the 'Unnamed Society'
   of Manchester by L. Oppenheimer at Lomax St., Salford,
   Manchester (with Lord Dunsany's *Fame And The Poet*).

Cast:

  1st Soldier: John Marchant
  2nd Soldier: P. J. C. Thornley
  The Queen: Beatrix Preston
  Amyntor: L. Oppenheimer
  Rhodope: Angela Lopez
  Phoenix: J. Wardle

Note: six performances in all. The second soldier is as above, and not A. H. Hilton as in the programme.

3. January 30, 1925: production of the 'Unnamed Society' of Manchester by L. Oppenheimer at Sandon Studios, Bluecoat Chambers, Liverpool (with Harold Brighouse's *The Apple Tree*). Cast: as No. 2 above.
Note: one performance only.

4. April 29, 1925: there was possibly a performance on this date at Wilmslow in Cheshire, but no details are known.

5. May 4, 1925: possibly a performance at Fargate, Sheffield (Y.M.C.A. Hall) on or soon after this date, but there are no details.

6. July 17 and 18, 1936: produced by A. K. Holland at the Sandon Studios, Bluecoat Chambers, Liverpool (with no other play).

Cast:

  1st Soldier: William Holford
  2nd Soldier: Trevor Thomas
  The Queen: Doreen Barker
  Amyntor: Harold Brown
  Rhodope: Nancy Nuttall
  Phoenix: Gwynn Davies

Note: two performances only.

(21)   STRATFORD-UPON-AVON REPORT

First edition:

1923   STRATFORD-*upon*-AVON | REPORT | on | Future Development | *Prepared, at the instance of the* | Stratford-*upon*-Avon *Preservation Committee, by* | PATRICK ABERCROMBIE & LASCELLES ABERCROMBIE | *Published by permission of the* Stratford-*upon*-Avon | Corporation, *the owners of the copyright* | *The* UNIVERSITY PRESS *of* LIVERPOOL *Ltd* | HODDER & STOUGHTON *Ltd* LONDON | 1923

Format: Royal 4to, 12¼ × 9¾ ins.

Collation: xii + 36 pages, consisting of:—
half-title, verso blank (pp. i–ii); title page, imprint on verso (pp. iii–iv); *Note* (pp. v–vi); *Preface* (pp. vii–viii); *Contents of the Report, List of plates* on verso (pp. ix–x); *Stratford-upon-Avon diagrams*, verso blank (pp. xi–xii); pages 1–35, text; page 36 blank.

Binding: (i) buff card; black lettering on front cover and spine; red end papers; photographic plates face pages 1, 4, 5, 8, 9, 30, and follow pages 4 and 28; diagrams face the title page, and pages 6, 17, 20, and 24; all edges uncut. (ii) red buckram; red leather spine and corners; gilt lettering and five fleur-de-lys ornaments on spine; single gilt lines on border of leather on front and outside back covers; red marbled end papers; photographic plates and diagrams as in binding (i); top edges of leaves gilt; fore and lower edges uncut.

Signatures: A^6 B–E^4 F^2.

Publication Date: September, 1923 [binding (i): 7s. 6d.].

When Patrick Abercrombie was approached by the Stratford Corporation, he suggested to them that L. A. would be able to help him. The Corporation agreed, and L. A. was then asked. In a letter of July 18, 1921, L. A. says 'my brother Pat and I have been asked to report to Stratford-on-A. corporation on possible (industrial) developments of Stratford. . . .'. They went to Stratford on July 19 and were there for about a week.

(22)   THE THEORY OF POETRY

First edition:

1924   The Theory of Poetry | By Lascelles Abercrombie | London: Martin Secker | Number Five John Street | Adelphi mcmxxiv

Format: Crown 8vo, $7\frac{1}{2} \times 5\frac{1}{2}$ ins.

Collation: 224 pages, consisting of:—
half-title, note [*By the same Author*] and imprint on verso (pp. 1–2); title page, *Preface* signed by L. A. ['The University, Leeds'] on verso (pp. 3–4); *Contents*, verso blank (pp. 5–6); pages 7–223, text; imprint on page 223; page 224 blank.

Binding: buff boards; yellow cloth spine; black lettering on spine; white end papers; top of leaves dyed black; fore and lower edges uncut.

Signatures: A^8 B–O^8.

Publication Date: February, 1924 [5s.].

Contents:

Introductory
Inspiration and Form
Technique
Diction: The Meaning of Words
Diction: The Sound of Words
The Poetic World

According to the preface, this was based on public lectures given in Liverpool and Leeds between October, 1920, and October, 1923. The final lectures that the book was primarily based upon were six given to the Leeds Literary and Philosophical Society (prepared around October 13, 1923) on October 24, 31, November 7, 14, 21, 28, 1923. Pages 139–146 were revised and expanded from pages 10–12 of *Poetry and Contemporary Speech*, q.v. (**13**).

A second impression was issued in January, 1926, with the title page: The Theory of Poetry | By Lascelles Abercrombie | *SECOND IMPRESSION* | London: Martin Secker | Number Five John Street | Adelphi mcmxxvi. The collation of the preliminaries for this impression: half-title, note [*By the same Author*] on verso (pp. 1–2); title page, note on publication and imprint on verso (pp. 3–4); *Contents, Preface* on verso (pp. 5–6). . . .

1,000 copies were printed of both impressions.

(23)   THE THEORY OF POETRY

Second edition: first American edition (combined binding):

1926   The Theory of Poetry | By Lascelles Abercrombie | [publisher's emblem] | New York | Harcourt, Brace and Company

Format: Demy 8vo, $8\frac{1}{8} \times 5\frac{3}{8}$ ins.

Collation: 338 pages, consisting of:—
blank leaf (the front end paper included in the pagination) (pp. 1–2); title page, imprint on verso (pp. 3–4); *Preface* signed by L. A. (pp. 5–8); *Contents*, verso blank (pp. 9–10); fly-title [*The Theory of Poetry*], verso blank (pp. 11–12); pages 13–170, text of *The Theory of Poetry*; fly-title [*The Idea of Great Poetry*], verso blank (pp. 171–172); pages 173–338, text of *The Idea of Great Poetry*.

Binding: blue cloth; yellow lettering on spine; impression of publisher's emblem on front cover; white end papers; fore and lower edges uncut.

Signatures: Unsigned: 1^{10} (-1^1) $2-21^8$.

Publication Date: January 14, 1926.

Contents: as the first edition (1924).

The first impression, of 1,500 copies, was printed in December, 1925; a second impression of 500 copies was printed in December, 1930.

The preface of this edition is completely different to either of the original edition's prefaces.

(24)   THE IDEA OF GREAT POETRY

First edition:

1925   The | Idea of Great Poetry | By Lascelles Abercrombie | London: Martin Secker | Number Five John Street | Adelphi mcmxxv

Format: Crown 8vo, $7\frac{1}{2} \times 5\frac{1}{2}$ ins.

Collation: 232 pages, consisting of:—
half-title, note [*By the same Author*] on verso (pp. 1-2); title page, *Preface* signed by L. A. on verso (pp. 3-4); *Contents*, verso blank (pp. 5-6); pages 7-232, text; imprint on page 232.

Binding: buff boards; yellow cloth spine; black lettering on spine; white end papers; top of leaves dyed black; fore and lower edges uncut.

Signatures: A^8 $B-O^8$ P^4.

Publication Date: June, 1925 [6s.].

Contents:

> Diction and Experience. Moments of Greatness.
> Greatness of Form. Refuge and Interpretation.
> Ideas and Persons.
> Tragic Greatness: The Hero.
> Poetic Personality. The Poet Himself.

This is a sequel to 'An Essay Towards a Theory of Art', q.v. (**17**), and 'The Theory of Poetry', q.v. (**22**). It was derived by revising and reducing the twelve Clark Lectures given at Trinity College, University of Cambridge, on October 19, 20, 26, 27, November 2, 3, 9, 10, 16, 17, 23, 24, 1923. By November 14, 1924, he had written half the book, and it was probably from the notes of the book that he delivered the five Ballard Matthews Lectures at the University College of North Wales, Bangor, on November 24, 25, 26, December 1, 2, 1924.

A second impression was issued in August, 1925, with the same collation, the title page being: The | Idea of Great Poetry | By Lascelles Abercrombie | *SECOND IMPRESSION* | London: Martin Secker | Number Five John Street | Adelphi mcmxxv. A third impression, issued in June, 1926, had the preliminaries changed to: half-title, note [*By the same Author*] on verso (pp. 1–2); title page, note on publication and imprint on verso (pp. 3–4); *Contents, Preface* signed by L. A. on verso (pp. 5–6); . . . The title page is: The | Idea of Great Poetry | By Lascelles Abercrombie | *THIRD IMPRESSION* | London: Martin Secker | Number Five John Street | Adelphi mcmxxvi.

(25)   THE IDEA OF GREAT POETRY

Second edition: first American edition (combined binding):

1926   The Theory of Poetry | By Lascelles Abercrombie | [publisher's emblem] | New York | Harcourt, Brace and Company

Format: Demy 8vo, $8\frac{1}{8} \times 5\frac{3}{8}$ ins.

Collation: 338 pages, consisting of:—

blank leaf (actually front end paper included in the pagination) (pp. 1–2); title page, imprint on verso (pp. 3–4); *Preface* signed by L. A. (pp. 5–8); *Contents*, verso blank (pp. 9–10); fly-title [*The Theory of Poetry*], verso blank (pp. 11–12); pages 13–170, text of *The Theory of Poetry*; fly-title [*The Idea of Great Poetry*], verso blank (pp. 171–172); pages 173–338, text of *The Idea of Great Poetry*.

Binding: blue cloth; yellow lettering on spine; impression of publisher's emblem on front cover; white end papers; fore and lower edges uncut.

Signatures: Unsigned: 1^{10} (-1^1) $2-21^8$.

Publication Date: January 14, 1926.

Contents: as the first edition (1925).

The first impression, of 1,500 copies, was printed in December, 1925; a second impression of 500 copies was printed in December, 1930.

The preface of this edition is completely different to either of the original edition's prefaces.

(26)   ROMANTICISM

First edition:

1926   Romanticism | By Lascelles Abercrombie | London: Martin Secker | Number Five John Street | Adelphi mcmxxvi

Format: Crown 8vo, $7\frac{1}{2} \times 5\frac{5}{8}$ ins.

Collation: 192 pages, consisting of:—
half-title, note [*By the same Author*] on verso (pp. 1–2); title page, imprint on verso (pp. 3–4); *Preface* signed by L. A. (pp. 5–7); *Contents* on page 8; pages 9–192, text; imprint on page 192.

Binding: buff boards; yellow cloth spine; black lettering on spine; white end papers; top of leaves dyed black; fore and lower edges uncut.

Signatures: A^8 B–M^8.

Publication Date: July, 1926 [6s.].

This was revised and expanded from three lectures given to Birkbeck College, University of London, on February 8, 15, 22, 1926. The first lecture was derived from an article in the *Times Literary Supplement* written by L. A. and entitled 'Views and Fairies', q.v. (**607**). The second lecture contains 186 lines translated by L. A. from ΚΑΘΑΡΜΟΙ (*Purifications*) by Empedocles, being interspersed with blank verse by L. A.

A second impression was issued in January, 1927, with the title page: Romanticism | By Lascelles Abercrombie | *SECOND IM-PRESSION* | London: Martin Secker | Number Five John Street | Adelphi mcmxxvii.

In 1927 an impression was issued in the U.S.A. by the Viking Press bound in grey cloth; red lettering on spine; impression of publisher's emblem on front cover; white end papers; fore and lower edges uncut. The title page is: Romanticism | By Lascelles Abercrombie | [publisher's emblem] | The Viking Press | New York mcmxxvii.

(27)   ROMANTICISM

Second edition:

1963   ROMANTICISM | by | Lascelles Abercrombie | London | HIGH HILL BOOKS

Format: Crown 8vo, $7\frac{1}{4} \times 4\frac{3}{4}$ ins.

Collation: 144 pages, consisting of:—
blank leaf (pp. 1–2); half-title, note and list of principal works on verso (pp. 3–4); title page, imprint on verso (pp. 5–6); *Contents, Publishers' Note* on verso (pp. 7–8); *Preface* signed by L. A. (pp. 9–11); page 12 blank; pages 13–142, text; blank leaf (pp. 143–144).

Binding: blue Linson; gilt lettering on spine; white end papers; all edges cut.

Signatures: A^8 B–I^8.

Publication Date: September 2, 1963 [18s.].

Distributed in the U.S.A. by Barnes and Noble, Inc., New York (published in the U.S.A. on October 5, 1963). 2,000 copies were printed.

(28)   TWELVE IDYLS AND OTHER POEMS

First edition:

1928   Twelve Idyls | And Other Poems | By Lascelles Abercrombie | London: Martin Secker | Number Five John Street | Adelphi mcmxxviii

Format: Crown 8vo, $7\frac{1}{2} \times 5\frac{1}{2}$ ins.

Collation: 200 pages, consisting of:—
half-title, note [*By the same Author*] on verso (pp. 1–2); title page, imprint on verso (pp. 3–4); dedication [*To Elizabeth And Robert Trevelyan*], verso blank (pp. 5–6); *Contents*, verso blank (pp. 7–8); fly-title [*Mary and the Bramble*], secondary dedication [*To my Mother*] on verso (pp. 9–10); pages 11–197, text; imprint on page 198; blank leaf (pp. 199–200).

Binding: buff boards; yellow cloth spine; black lettering on spine; white end papers; top of leaves dyed black; fore and lower edges uncut.

Signatures: A^8 B–M^8 N^4.

Publication Date: October (10?), 1928 [6s.].

Contents: IDYLS.

Mary and the Bramble (page 11)
For notes on this poem, see main entry (**3**).

The Innocents (page 23)
A poem of 135 lines; it is uncertain when it was written, but it was probably immediately prior to its publication in *New Numbers*, q.v. (**563**). It was completely revised from 162 lines in *New Numbers* for this book.

The Death of a Friar (page 33)
A poem of 265 lines; it was written *c.* 1926–27.

At Endor (page 49)

A dramatic poem of 144 lines. It was planned, but not started, by February 11, 1908. Originally called 'Witch at Endor', and then 'Witchcraft: Old Style'; he probably finished writing it by 1914, but between April 13 and 17, 1919, it was completely recast. In 1923 it was refused for an anthology, so he changed the name once more to 'At Endor', again completely revising it.

Witchcraft: New Style (page 59)

A dramatic poem of 159 lines. He began writing this on April 7, 1919, finishing it on April 13. Published in *Georgian Poetry, 1918–1919*, q.v. (**103**), being slightly revised for this book. There is no trace of it being published prior to publication in *Georgian Poetry*.

In the Dunes (page 69)

A dramatic poem of 281 lines. He began writing it on April 2, 1919, finishing on April 6. It was originally published in *Voices*, q.v. (**617**), with 282 lines, and also in *A Miscellany of Poetry*, q.v. (**105**) with 282 lines (line six was completely omitted when it was published in *Twelve Idyls*).

The Six Men of Calais (page 85)

A dramatic poem of 107 lines; not known when it was written, but probably in 1911 or 1912. Originally published in the *Poetry Review*, q.v. (**585**), with 120 lines, being completely revised for this book.

Asmodeus in Egypt (page 95)

A poem of 306 lines; it was written *c.* 1926–27.

Ham and Eggs (page 113)

A dramatic poem of 417 lines. It was written on the following dates: May 17 to 25, June 4 to 5, and 11 to 17 (3.30 a.m.), 1919; given the finishing touches on June 20, 1919. Originally published in the *Chapbook*, q.v. (**218**), dated May, 1919, with 418 lines. Slightly revised for this book.

Ryton Firs (page 135)

The prelude is a 14 stanza poem of 56 lines. Written on April 27 and 28, 1919, the first two stanzas being written last. The remainder ('Ryton Firs I'; there was to have been a 'Ryton Firs II' added to the remainder, but it was never written) is a poem of 190 lines which he began writing on April 29, and finished about May 3, 1919. Dedicated in this book 'For David, Michael, Ralph' (his three sons). It was originally published in the *Chapbook*, q.v. (**217**), with the prelude as 48 lines (12 stanzas), and the remainder as 163 lines. The Dance at the end of the remainder was to have been published in the *Sphere* (no trace can be found in this periodical), and therefore was deliberately omitted from inclusion in the *Chapbook*. The remainder only was later published in *Georgian Poetry, 1920–1922* taken directly from the *Chapbook*. A translation into French of a part of 'The Voices in a Dream' (lines 40 to 56 of the remainder, as published in the *Chapbook*) by Emile B. d'Erlanger was published on a broadsheet, $9\frac{3}{8} \times 7$ ins. It is undated, and it is not known why it was produced.

The Olympians (page 149)

A dramatic poem of 580 lines; he probably finished writing this in January or February, 1914, just before publication in *New Numbers*, q.v. (**561**). It was completely revised from 704 lines in *New Numbers* for inclusion in this book.

Zagreus (page 179)

A poem of 156 lines; originally an extremely long poem (unknown number of lines), written July to August, 1913. After he had read it to Edward Marsh who fell asleep before he had finished, it was drastically revised and reduced from its original in the winter of 1920–21.

MISCELLANEOUS

Inscriptions (page 189)

A poem of 12 lines, in three stanzas numbered I to III. It was written late, 1920, and dedicated: I, For the Roll of Honour of the University of Liverpool; II, For the First Anniversary of the Armistice; III, For the War Memorial of the Liverpool Post Office. The second stanza originally appeared in the *Liverpool Chapbook*, q.v. (**262**).

R. B. (page 191)

A poem of three stanzas, 13 lines. Written about Rupert Brooke, probably in April or May, 1915, soon after Brooke's death.

White Love (Out of Sidi Hammo) (page 192)

A poem of 10 lines; probably written just before December 25, 1908. Originally published in the *Microcosm*, q.v. (**541**), and later in *The Book of the Microcosm*, q.v. (**109**), before inclusion here.

The Nightingale (From the Old English Riddle) (page 193)

A poem of 11 lines; probably written late December, 1920, but possibly as early as November, 1918. It was based on the eighth riddle in the Exeter Book. Originally published in an article in the *Morning Post*, q.v. (**545**).

The Stream's Song (page 194)

A poem of nine stanzas, 36 lines. Probably written in 1910 or 1911.

Originally published in the *Vineyard*, q.v. (**615**), and slightly revised before a later inclusion in the *Daily Express*, q.v. (**221**). Published here without any further revision.

Elizabeth's Song (page 196)

A poem of two stanzas, 12 lines. Originally entitled 'A Girl's Song' when it was written about 1911 to 1914, but the name was changed after February, 1922, when his daughter Elizabeth was born. It was set to music by John Clements in 1942, and published in 1948, with the music sheet cover/title page: Elizabeth's Song | A Song for Soprano Voice | [ornament] | Poem by | Lascelles Abercrombie | Music by | John Clements | Key G | [F#–B] | 2/– net | KEITH PROWSE & C° LTD., | MUSIC PUBLISHERS | 159, NEW BOND STREET W.1. | PUBLISHING DEPT | 42–43, POLAND STREET, W.1. | LONDON | MADE IN ENGLAND [all except 'Made in England' in double line border].

Epitaph (page 197)

A poem of 14 lines; probably written in 1926.

L. A. was in essence a poet, and so it is obvious why he decided in August, 1918, to compile another book of poems. He said in a letter of August 14, 1918: 'My future plans shape themselves at present into three books . . . 1. A book of short mixed Idylls, "Mary" and "The Innocents" etc. 2. A book of perhaps four long metaphysical Idylls, of which "The Olympians" is the type. 3. A book of short plays, "The Staircase", "End of the World" etc.' [see *Four Short Plays* (**18**)].

On April 2, 1919, he went back to Dymock in Gloucestershire from Liverpool, to stay with his friend Roland Hyett at 'Crowfield', leaving his wife and three boys in Grange-over-Sands, Lancashire. His sole reason was to write poetry for the books. He wrote five 'Idyls' there, including both parts of 'Ryton Firs', and recast 'Witchcraft: Old Style' (published as 'At Endor').

Because he had given up writing poetry from 1920 until he became seriously ill in 1926, the book did not appear sooner. It was not until he was convalescing that he wrote another two 'Idyls', and his 'Epitaph'.

On March 13, 1928, he was able to write to Robert Trevelyan that he had started to compile the book – 'mostly old work which doesn't greatly please me: and revising is the devil'. On June 21, 1928, he sent the proofs to Trevelyan, at the same time asking him to be the dedicatee.

Probably 1,000 copies were printed; about 300 had been sold by the beginning of June, 1929.

First edition:

1929   PROGRESS | IN LITERATURE | BY | LASCELLES ABERCROMBIE | *Professor of English Literature* | *in the University* | *of Leeds* | THE LESLIE STEPHEN LECTURE | DELIVERED AT CAMBRIDGE | 10 MAY 1929 | CAMBRIDGE | *At the University Press* | 1929

Format: Crown 8vo, (i) $7\frac{3}{8} \times 4\frac{7}{8}$ ins. (ii) $6\frac{1}{2} \times 4\frac{1}{2}$ ins.

Collation (i): $ii + 54$ pages, consisting of:—
blank leaf (pasted to inside front cover) (pp. i–ii); half-title, imprint on verso (pp. 1–2); title page (in ornamental border), imprint on verso (pp. 3–4); pages 5–53, text; imprint on page 54.

Binding (i): grey paper wrapper; black lettering on spine, and on front cover in ornamental border; white end paper at the back; all edges cut.

Collation (ii): $ii + 54$ pages, consisting of:—
As collation (i), except blank leaf not pasted to inside front cover.

Binding (ii): grey boards; black lettering on spine, and on front cover in ornamental border; white end papers; all edges cut.

Signatures: $A1^4$ A2–A7^4.

Publication Date: May 11, 1929 [2s. 6d.].

This was published a day after the lecture was delivered; he says in a letter of March 24, 1929: 'I had to set about my Leslie Stephen lecture: tho' it isn't to be actually delivered before May 10, it has to be printed before that'.

1,000 copies were printed. It was distributed in the U.S.A. by Macmillan of New York (probably published the same date).

(30)   THE POEMS OF
                  LASCELLES ABERCROMBIE

First edition:

1930   *The Poems of* | LASCELLES | ABERCROMBIE | [ornament] | LONDON | OXFORD UNIVERSITY PRESS | HUMPHREY MILFORD | 1930

Format: Crown 8vo, $7\frac{1}{8} \times 4\frac{7}{8}$ ins.

Collation: 2+x+552 pages, consisting of:—
blank leaf (pp. 1–2); half-title, verso blank (pp. i–ii); title page, imprint on verso (pp. iii–iv); *Preface* signed by L. A. (pp. v–vii); page viii, blank; *Contents* (pp. ix–x); fly-title [*Poems*], verso blank (pp. 1–2); pages 3–550, text; imprint, verso blank (pp. 551–552).

Binding: (i) blue cloth; gilt lettering and ornament on spine and front cover; white end papers; top edges of leaves gilt; fore and lower edges uncut; photograph of L. A. by Emery Walker, Ltd. with tissue protection facing title page. (ii) [First India paper state] red cloth; gilt lettering and single line border on spine and front cover; white end papers; gilt over red dye on all edges; all edges cut; photograph of L. A. by Emery Walker, Ltd. with tissue protection facing title page. (iii) [Second India paper state] blue cloth; gilt lettering on spine and front cover; white end papers; gilt over red dye on all edges; all edges cut; photograph of L. A. by Emery Walker, Ltd. with tissue protection facing title page. (iv) [fourth binding state, *c.* 1939] blue cloth; gilt lettering on spine; impression of publisher's emblem and single line border and panels on front cover; white end papers; top of leaves dyed pale blue; all edges cut. (v) [Third India paper state; *c.* 1939] blue cloth; gilt lettering on spine; impression of publisher's emblem and single line border and panels on front cover; white end papers; top of leaves dyed blue; all edges cut.

Signatures: A^6 B–S^{16} T^4.

Publication Date: October, 1930 [6s.].

Contents: POEMS.

This book is in the 'Oxford Poets' series. It contains every poem and play published before 1930 in principal books, except the verses in *Romanticism*; no new material has been added. All are in the versions of immediately prior to 1930. For notes on the poems, see the separate books.

According to the *English Catalogue of Books*, an edition of this book was published in 1930 as Demy 8vo, with 537 pages; no trace of this has been found.

(31)   THE SALE OF SAINT THOMAS

First (limited) edition:

1930   The Sale of Saint Thomas | *in Six Acts* | *by* | Lascelles Abercrombie | 1930 | [rule] | *London:* Martin Secker

Format: Royal 8vo, $9\frac{7}{8} \times 6\frac{1}{2}$ ins.

Collation: 128 pages, consisting of:—
blank leaf (pp. 1–2); half-title, verso blank (pp. 3–4); title page, *Note* signed by L. A. on verso (pp. 5–6); note [*This edition is limited to 480 numbered copies each signed by the author of which this is no. . . .*], verso blank (pp. 7–8); dedication [*To Arthur Ransome My Friend*], verso blank (pp. 9–10); notes [*The Tradition; The Persons; The Acts*], verso blank (pp. 11–12); fly-title [*I*], verso blank (pp. 13–14); pages 15–124, text; imprint, verso blank (pp. 125–126); blank leaf (pp. 127–128).

Binding: blue buckram; gilt lettering on spine; white end papers; top edges of leaves gilt; fore and lower edges uncut.

Signatures: A^8 B–H^8.

Publication Date: (December?), 1930 [15s.].

Contents: 'The Acts'
>   The Quay of an Arabian Port
>   On Shipboard
>   The Slave-shed
>   The King's Chamber
>   The Camp
>   The Palace

This is a dramatic poem, with the number of lines: Act I, 555; II, 347; III, 321; IV, 348; V, 288; IV, 831. The first act was originally published in pamphlet form in 1911, q.v. (**4**). It is not known when the other five acts were written, but he had probably been working at it, on and off, since 1926. The first 20 lines of the second act had previously appeared in the *Sea Microcosm*, q.v. (**III**).

53

On October 20, 1930, he said in a letter: 'I have taken the plunge, and handed over St. Thomas to Secker, who will send it to the printers tomorrow. The thing is not satisfactory as it stands: but it's hopeless to think of making it satisfactory, . . . and as long as I have it by me I keep on tinkering at it instead of doing the work I ought to be doing. It's a failure, but it's becoming an incubus: so I have decided to put it out of its misery. If there's a second edition I may improve it. It will be printed first in a limited edition at 15/–, and three months later reissued at 5/–: that's Secker's idea, and he has persuaded me to waive my objection to limited editions. I hope he won't drop money on it.' On November 6, L. A. received the proofs.

(32)   THE SALE OF SAINT THOMAS

First edition: second impression:

1930   The Sale of Saint Thomas | *in Six Acts* | *by* | Lascelles
[1931] Abercrombie | 1931 | [rule] | *London:* Martin Secker

Format: Crown 8vo, $7\frac{1}{2} \times 5$ ins.

Collation: 128 pages, consisting of:—
two blank leaves (pp. 1–4); half-title, verso blank (pp. 5–6); title page, *Note* signed by L. A. on verso (pp. 7–8); dedication [*To Arthur Ransome My Friend*], verso blank (pp. 9–10); notes [*The Tradition; The Persons; The Acts*], verso blank (pp. 11–12); fly-title [*I*], verso blank (pp. 13–14); pages 15–124, text; imprint, verso blank (pp. 125–126); blank leaf (pp. 127–128).

Binding: (i) brown cloth; gilt lettering on spine; white end papers; fore and lower edges uncut. (ii) [later binding state] brown cloth (lighter than (i)); red lettering on spine; white end papers; all edges cut.

Signatures: A^8 B–H^8.

Issued: November, 1931 [3s. 6d.].

Contents: As the first impression.
   Because of imperfections in the photographic blocks, made during copying, there were four mistakes in this impression in act VI: on page 100 (Act VI, line 148), full-stop missing after 'breathes'; (line 149), 'pier' should be 'piercing'; (line 151), 'mirr' should be 'mirror'; page 101 (line 170), 'P' missing from 'Physician'. L. A. had always objected to limited editions, but had been persuaded by Secker to allow that of

1930 to be published. Had there been no limited edition, the following unlimited impression would not have been produced by photocopy with its consequent imperfections. It may well be that this incident completed L. A.'s growing disenchantment with Secker and led to his leaving the publisher altogether.

(33)   PRINCIPLES OF LITERARY CRITICISM

First edition:

1932   PRINCIPLES OF | LITERARY CRITICISM | By | Prof. LASCELLES ABERCROMBIE | Professor of English Literature in the | University of London | LONDON | VICTOR GOLLANCZ LTD | 14 Henrietta Street Covent Garden | 1932

Format: Crown 8vo, $6\frac{7}{8} \times 4\frac{3}{4}$ ins.

Collation: 160 pages, consisting of:—
half-title, verso blank (pp. 1–2); title page, imprint on verso (pp. 3–4); *Contents*, verso blank (pp. 5–6); pages 7–159, text; *Bibliographical Note* on page 160.

Binding: (i) red card; black lettering on spine, and on front cover in double line border; advertisement on outside back cover; white end papers; all edges cut. (ii) red paper wrapper; black lettering on spine, and on front cover in double line border; advertisement on outside back cover; no end papers; all edges cut.

Signatures: Ac^8 Bc–Kc^8.

Publication Date: September 12, 1932 [1s. 6d.].

Contents:

> Introductory
> The Art of Literature
> Aristotle's 'Poetics'
> After Aristotle
> Conclusion

This is possibly based on ten lectures L. A. gave to Bedford College, London, on October 15, 22, 29, November 5, 12, 19, 26, December 3, 10, 17, 1930.

This edition is in the 'Outline Series', having been originally published in *An Outline of Modern Knowledge*, q.v. (**116**).

A second impression was issued in May, 1935, with the note 'second edition' on the verso of the title page, and the date omitted from the title page.

(34)   PRINCIPLES OF LITERARY CRITICISM

First edition: third impression:

1932   PRINCIPLES OF | LITERARY CRITICISM | by |
[1961] Lascelles Abercrombie | London | HIGH HILL BOOKS

> *Format:* Crown 8vo, $7\frac{1}{4} \times 4\frac{7}{8}$ ins.
>
> *Collation:* 160 pages, consisting of:—
> half-title, verso blank (pp. 1–2); title page, imprint on verso (pp. 3–4);
> *Contents,* verso blank (pp. 5–6); pages 7–159, text; page 160 blank.
>
> *Binding:* (i) grey Linson; gilt lettering on spine; white end papers; all
> edges cut. (ii) [second binding state, December, 1966] white card
> wrapper; blue lettering on spine and front cover; note [*scholarly books
> of related interest*] on outside back cover; no end papers; all edges cut;
> dust cover pasted to inside of card wrapper.
>
> *Signatures:* Ac^8 Bc–Kc^8.
>
> *Issued:* January 9, 1961 (erroneously dated 1960) [12s. 6d.].
>
> *Contents:* as the first impression.
>
> Distributed in the U.S.A. by Barnes and Noble of New York
> (issued in the U.S.A. on February 28, 1961, also erroneously dated
> 1960). 2,000 copies were printed.

(35)   PRINCIPLES OF LITERARY CRITICISM

First Indian (English) edition:

1958   PRINCIPLES OF | LITERARY CRITICISM | By |
        LASCELLES ABERCROMBIE | Professor of English
        Literature in the | University of London | [publisher's
        emblem] | VORA & CO., PUBLISHERS Private LTD. |
        3 Round Building, Bombay 2.

> *Format:* Crown 8vo, $7\frac{1}{4} \times 4\frac{3}{4}$ ins.
>
> *Collation:* 160 pages, consisting of:—
> half-title, verso blank (pp. 1–2); title page, imprints on verso (pp. 3–4);
> *Contents,* verso blank (pp. 5–6); pages 7–159, text; *Bibliographical Note*
> on page 160.
>
> *Binding:* white paper boards; red lettering and publisher's emblem on
> spine; reverse lettering (red cover with white lettering) on front
> cover; white end papers; all edges cut.
>
> *Signatures:* P–1^8 P–2 – P–10^8.
>
> *Publication Date:* 1958 [Rs. 3.75].
>
> *Contents:* as the first edition (1932).

This edition was also published in Hindi (1,500 copies, first impression), and Gujurati (1,000 copies, first impression). Neither of these has been examined.

(36) PRINCIPLES OF LITERARY CRITICISM

Second Indian edition:

1964 [translation:] Principles of Literary Criticism | [in English] (Principles of Literary Criticism | Original: | Lascelles Abercrombie | Translation: | C. P. K. | Karnataka Co-operative Publishing House, by order | Chamaraja Pet, Bangalore-18

Format: Demy 8vo, $8\frac{1}{2} \times 5\frac{1}{2}$ ins.

Collation: $vi + 88$ pages, consisting of:—
title page, imprint and notes on publication on verso (pp. i–ii); *Contents*, verso blank (pp. iii–iv); *Our Words* signed by K. V. Shankara Gowda, President, June 30, 1964, *Foreword* signed by the translator C. P. Krishnakumar, at Mysore, June 1964 on verso (pp. v–vi); pages 1–86, text; *Bibliographical Note* in English, verso blank (pp. 87–88).

Binding: pale green card wrapper; blue lettering within double line border on front cover; no end papers; all edges cut.

Signatures: π^4 $(-\pi 3)$ 1^8 $2 - 5^8$ 6^4.

Publication Date: (August?), 1964 [Rs. 1.75].

Contents: as the first edition (1932).

The language of this edition is Kannada. It was erroneously dated June, 1964.

(37) PRINCIPLES OF LITERARY CRITICISM

First Arabic edition:

? [translation:] Committee for Editions, Translations and Publications | [rule] | Digest of Modern Knowledge Number 3 | [broken rule] | Principles of Literary Criticism | [short rule] | by | Lascelles Abercrombie | [in English] Lascelles Abercrombie | Professor of English Literature, University of London | [short rule] | Translated into

Arabic | by | Dr. Mohamad Awad Mohamed | Assistant Professor in the Faculty of Arts | [rule] | General Knowledge Series | Committee for Editions, Translations and Publications Press | 1936

Format: Demy 8vo, $7\frac{3}{4} \times 5\frac{3}{8}$ ins.

Collation: (this book is taken, when relating to a European book, as reading backwards; i.e. the title page is at the back of the book, and the verso of a page in this book would be the recto of a page in a European book).

$vi + 186$ pages, consisting of:—
title page (all except publisher and date within triple line border), verso blank (pp. i–ii); *Contents*, verso blank (pp. iii–iv); fly-title, verso blank (pp. v–vi); pages 1–186, text.

Binding: green wrapper; green lettering on front and outside back covers; no end papers; all edges cut.

Signatures: Unsigned: $1 - 12^8$.

Publication Date: not known.

Contents: as the first edition (1932).

The date on the title page is apparently not the date of publication, but the date the publishers were founded. It is probable, however, that this was published near this date or in the 1940's.

(38)   POETRY: ITS MUSIC AND MEANING

First edition:

1932   *Poetry:* | ITS MUSIC AND MEANING | *By* | Lascelles Abercrombie | [ornament] | *London* | OXFORD UNIVERSITY PRESS | HUMPHREY MILFORD | 1932

Format: Crown 8vo, $7\frac{1}{2} \times 5\frac{1}{8}$ ins.

Collation: 64 pages, consisting of:—
half-title, verso blank (pp. 1–2); title page, imprint on verso (pp. 3–4); *Preface* signed by L. A., verso blank (pp. 5–6); *Contents*, verso blank (pp. 7–8); pages 9–64, text; imprint on page 64.

Binding: (i) orange paper wrapper; dark blue lettering within ornamental border on front cover; advertisement on outside back cover; no end papers; fore and lower edges uncut. (ii) [later binding state] green cloth; black lettering on spine; white end papers; all edges cut.

Signatures: A^4 B–H^4.

Publication Date: November 24, 1932 [2s.].
Approximately 5,000 copies were printed.

(39)   TO SIR WALFORD DAVIES

First edition:

1934   *To* —— [line in blue] | *Sir Walford Davies* | *at Gregynog* | *June, 1934*

Format: (i) $16\frac{1}{2} \times 9\frac{1}{2}$ ins., broadsheet. (ii) $15\frac{1}{2} \times 9\frac{1}{2}$ ins., broadsheet; the title is omitted, and it is produced on less expensive paper. Both formats were produced simultaneously.

Publication Date: June (18?), 1934.

This broadsheet was printed by the Gregynog Press for private circulation at the Gregynog Festival, to commemorate the appointment of Sir Walford Davies to the 'Master of the King's Musick', in April, 1934. It was read by L. A. to the festival on June 18, 1934.

The poem was written *c.* May to June, 1934. The broadsheet was unsigned, but the poem, of 47 lines, was reprinted in the *Listener*, q.v. (**258**), and later in *Lyrics and Unfinished Poems*, q.v. (**40**).

(40)   LYRICS AND UNFINISHED POEMS

First edition:

1940   LYRICS | AND | UNFINISHED POEMS | BY | LASCELLES ABERCROMBIE | THE GREGYNOG PRESS | MCMXL

Format: Demy 4to, $11\frac{1}{4} \times 7\frac{5}{8}$ ins.

Collation: $8 + $ xii $ + 96$ pages, consisting of:—
four blank leaves (pp. 1–8); half-title, verso blank (pp. i–ii); title page, verso blank (pp. iii–iv); *Foreword* (pp. v–vi); *A Note on the Poetry of Lascelles Abercrombie* signed by Wilfrid Gibson (pp. vii–xi); *The Contents* (p. xii); fly-title [*Lyrics*], verso blank (pp. 1–2); pages 3–82, text; note [*Of this edition hand-set in the 'Romulus' type of Messrs. Enschedé en Zonen, one hundred and seventy-five copies have been printed under the direction of James Wardrop, on Barcham Green hand-made paper at the Gregynog Press, near Newtown, Montgomeryshire. Finished on the twenty-eighth day of June, mcmxl. No. . . .*], verso blank (pp. 83–84); six blank leaves (pp. 85–96).

Binding: (i) Douglas Cockerell combed marbled boards; dark green leather spine; gilt lettering and vertical lines on spine; pages *1–4* and *93–96* used as end papers; fore and lower edges uncut. (ii) blue-green leather; gilt lettering and lines on spine; gilt lines on front and outside back covers (designed by George Fisher); pages 1–4 and 93–96 used as end papers; top edges of leaves gilt; fore and lower edges uncut.

Signatures: $\pi^4\ A^6$ B–M^4 N^4.

Publication Date: August 10, 1940 [(i) 25s.; (ii) 10 gns.].

Contents: LYRICS

This World of Terrible Beauty (page 3)

> A poem of four stanzas, 18 lines. Written for his wife's birthday on April 13, 1912.

The Future (page 4)

> A poem of four stanzas, 16 lines. It is not known when this was written, but probably between 1911 and 1914.

April 13th, 1908 (page 5)

> A three stanza poem of 12 lines. This was actually written in 1906, probably for April 13, the birthday of Catherine Gwatkin. The poem that was written for April 13, 1908, was 'Epilogue: Dedication' in *Emblems of Love.*

April 13th, 1915 (page 6)

> A poem of six stanzas, 24 lines; written for his wife's birthday. It was previously published in the *Times Literary Supplement,* q.v. (**606**), with the last stanza omitted, under the title 'The Lover in Wartime'.

I Have No Fear of Death (page 8)

> A two stanza poem of eight lines. It is not known when this was written, but probably between 1911 and 1914.

Skyros (page 9)

> A poem of ten lines. Probably written in 1931 when he went to the Greek isle of this name for the unveiling of a statue to Rupert Brooke.

Down To the Ground Like a Stone (page 10)

> A poem of seven lines. Written sometime between 1911 and 1914.

Hokku: Colours In Herefordshire (page 11)

> Two separate poems of three lines each. It is likely both were written in August, 1910.

My Stick (page 12)

A poem of 37 lines. Probably written between 1911 and 1914.

Praise of Thirst (page 14)

A two stanza poem of 12 lines. Uncertain when written, but is likely to have been between 1911 and 1914.

For Bicycling (page 15)

A poem of two stanzas, eight lines. Written on or about February 6, 1912.

An Ode To Sir Walford Davies (page 16)

For notes on this poem, see main entry (39).

UNFINISHED POEMS

The Just Godfather (page 21)

A dramatic poem of 265 lines. Written sometime between 1911 and 1914.

Fragment of a Philosophical Poem (page 34)

A poem of two parts, with the number of lines: Part I, 102; II, 59 Probably written between 1923 and 1929.

The Shepherds (page 41)

A poetic drama of 640 lines (Act I only is included). Most likely written in 1918.

Fragments From Y Tryfan (page 76)

A poem of 42 lines. It is not known when it was written, although it is possible, but unlikely, to have been written as early as 1907.

Two Fragments From Alfred (page 78)

The number of lines of the fragments are: I (The sudden burst of Danes' war on Alfred's establisht kingdom), 10; II (Battlefield in truce), 8. Probably written between 1911 and 1914.

Fragments of an Ode: ΠΟΛΛΑ ΤΕ ΔΕΙΝΑ (page 79)

22 lines of fragments. Written sometime between 1911 and 1914.

[Fragments] (page 80)

Nine untitled fragments of poems with the number of lines: No. I, 4; II, 4; III, 4; IV, 6; V, 4; VI, 6; VII, 3; VIII, 10; IX, 4. They were all probably written between 1911 and 1914.

Ralph Abercrombie and Robert Trevelyan collected the poems together, and R. A. wrote the Foreword. Catherine Abercrombie was paid £20 for the rights of publication of the poems.

Numbers 1 to 20 were 'De Luxe' bound, the remainder being 'Standard' bound.

First edition:

1952 THE ART OF | WORDSWORTH | [ornament] | *Lascelles Abercrombie* | GEOFFREY CUMBERLEGE | OXFORD UNIVERSITY PRESS | *London New York Toronto* | 1952

Format: Crown 8vo, $7\frac{1}{2} \times 4\frac{3}{4}$ ins.

Collation: viii + 160 pages, consisting of:—
half-title, verso blank (pp. i–ii); title page, imprint on verso (pp. iii–iv); *Prefatory Note* signed by Ralph Abercrombie (pp. v–vi); *Contents*, verso blank (pp. vii–viii); pages 1–154, text; *Index* (pp. 155–157); imprint on page 158; blank leaf (pp. 159–160).

Binding: red cloth; gilt lettering on spine; white end papers; lower edges uncut.

Signatures: A^4 B–L^8.

Publication Date: April 17, 1952 [10s. 6d.].

Contents:

    Introductory
    Inspiration
    Construction
    Diction
    Value
    Appendix: 'Peter Bell'

This book was edited by Ralph Abercrombie, L. A.'s son, from a number of lectures. The original lectures, given in 1931 to the University of Belfast, were elaborated on for a series of lectures given on April 4, 8, 9, 11, 15, 1935, to the Percy Turnbull Foundation at the Johns Hopkins University, Baltimore, U.S.A. This also included material from a previous lecture on 'Peter Bell', probably revised from the original lectures given in Paris on February 7 and 9, 1927.

The book had been planned as early as March, 1939. Approximately 2,000 copies were printed.

First edition: second (American) impression:

1952 THE ART OF | WORDSWORTH | [ornament] |

[1965] *Lascelles Abercrombie* | ARCHON BOOKS | HAMDEN, CONNECTICUT | 1965

Format: Crown 8vo, $7\frac{1}{2} \times 5$ ins.

Collation: viii + 160 pages, consisting of:—
half-title, verso blank (pp. i–ii); title page, imprint on verso (pp. iii–iv); *Prefatory Note* signed by Ralph Abercrombie (pp. v–vi); *Contents,* verso blank (pp. vii–viii); pages 1–154, text; *Index* (pp. 155–157); page 158 blank; blank leaf (pp. 159–160).

Binding: blue cloth; gilt lettering on spine; white end papers; all edges cut.

Signatures: A^4 B–L^8.

Issued: February 5, 1965 [$5.00].

Contents: as the first impression.
  1,000 copies were printed.

(43)   VISION AND LOVE

First edition:

1966 VISION AND | LOVE | LASCELLES ABERCROMBIE | LONDON: | ARts Research

Format: Demy 8vo, $8\frac{5}{8} \times 5\frac{3}{4}$ ins.

Collation: 16 unnumbered pages, consisting of:—
blank leaf (pp. 1–2); title page, note [*This booklet of nine previously unpublished poems is produced for the 85th birthday of Catherine Abercrombie: Wednesday, April 13th, 1966; being restricted to 25 copies*] and imprint on verso (pp. 3–4); *Contents,* verso blank (about five copies have a line across the top of the page) (pp. 5–6); pages 7–15, text; page 16 blank.

Binding: red card wrapper; black lettering on front cover; imprint on outside back cover; no end papers; all edges cut.

Signatures: None (one gathering).

Publication Date: See note below.

Contents (all poem titles in red):
Vision (page 7)

An eight line poem of two stanzas. Probably written about 1903; he says in a letter in December, 1906 that it was 'a song I made some years ago'.

Soul's Element (page 8)
A four line poem; written on June 4, 1907.

Destiny (page 9)
A two stanza poem of twelve lines.   Written on February 25, 1908.

The Alps (page 10)
A two stanza poem of eight lines. Written while his fiancée, Catherine Gwatkin, was on holiday in Switzerland, on June 14, 1908.

The Dramatist (page 11)
A twenty line poem of five stanzas; it was written on June 29, 1908. Sent for publication in the *Nation* the following day, but was refused.

Love (page 12)
A four line poem; probably written in late 1908 as a fragment of a larger poem, possibly 'Marriage Song' (See *Emblems of Love* [5]).

Joy (page 13)
A four line poem. This may have been written as a fragment of a longer poem, possibly 'Marriage Song', in late 1908.

Night (page 14)
A five line poem, likely to have been written early 1922.

Morning Song for David (page 15)
A nine stanza poem of 36 lines. Written on or about April 13, 1911. This booklet was not for sale, and therefore was not given a publication date, but it was received from the printers on June 17, 1966. 28 copies were printed.

CONTRIBUTIONS TO BOOKS, ETC.

Georgian Poetry 1911–1912
Georgian Poetry 1913–1915
Georgian Poetry 1918–1919
Georgian Poetry 1920–1922
A Miscellany of Poetry 1920–1922
The Encyclopædia Britannica
Great Names
Babel
The Book of the Microcosm
The Iliad of Homer
The Sea-Microcosm
Poems by Nicholas Nekrassov
Friends in Solitude
George W. Harris
Hommage a Rupert Brooke
An Outline of Modern Knowledge
New English Poems
S. P. E. Tract No. XXXVI
Revaluations
Hommage a Rupert Brooke 1887 1915
The Eighteen-Sixties
Ten Contemporaries
The Great Victorians
Selected Modern English Essays
The Letters of W. Dixon Scott
Aspects of Shakespeare
Edwardian England
English Critical Essays
Some Appreciations of William Morris
Lady Precious Stream
Catalogue . . . of Works by Ernest Proctor
The Collected Poems of John Drinkwater
The Dictionary of National Biography
Leeds University Verse Anthology

---

(101)   GEORGIAN POETRY 1911–1912

1912 GEORGIAN | POETRY | 1911–1912 | [three ornaments]
| [two ornaments] | [one ornament] | THE POETRY
BOOKSHOP | 35 DEVONSHIRE ST. THEOBALDS
RD | LONDON W.C.

Format: viii+200 pages; Double-Crown 16mo, $7\frac{3}{4} \times 5$ ins., fore and
lower edges uncut. Buff boards.

66

Publication Date: December, 1912.

Contribution: *The Sale of Saint Thomas* on pages 3–21. It was previously published in pamphlet form, q.v. (**4**), where notes on this poem will be found.

This publication was edited by Edward Marsh, as were all editions of *Georgian Poetry.*

(**102**)   GEORGIAN POETRY 1913–1915

1915   GEORGIAN | POETRY | 1913–1915 | [three ornaments] | [two ornaments] | [one ornament] | THE POETRY BOOKSHOP | 35 DEVONSHIRE ST. THEOBALDS RD. | LONDON W.C. | MCMXV

Format: $x+246$ pages; Double-Crown 16mo, $7\frac{3}{4} \times 5$ ins., fore and lower edges uncut. Blue boards.

Publication Date: December, 1915.

Contribution: *The End of the World* on pages 195–239. Previously published in *New Numbers*, q.v. (**562**); later published in *Four Short Plays*, q.v. (**18**) where notes on this play will be found.

(**103**)   GEORGIAN POETRY 1918–1919

1919   GEORGIAN | POETRY | 1918–1919 | [three ornaments] | [two ornaments] | [one ornament] | THE POETRY BOOKSHOP | 35 Devonshire Street | Theobalds Road | W.C. | MCMXIX

Format: $x+198$ pages; Crown 8vo, $7\frac{1}{2} \times 5$ ins., fore and lower edges uncut. Orange boards.

Publication Date: November, 1919.

Contribution: *Witchcraft: New Style* on pages 3–7. It is not known where it was previously published, if it was. Later published in *Twelve Idyls and Other Poems*, q.v. (**28**), where notes on this poem will be found.

(**104**)   GEORGIAN POETRY 1920–1922

1922   GEORGIAN | POETRY | 1920–1922 | [three ornaments] | [two ornaments] | [one ornament] | THE POETRY

BOOKSHOP | 35 DEVONSHIRE ST. THEOBALDS RD. | LONDON W.C.1 | MCMXXII

Format: xiv + 210 pages; Crown 8vo, $7\frac{1}{2} \times 5$ ins., fore and lower edges uncut. Red boards.

Publication Date: November, 1922.

Contribution: *Ryton Firs* on pages 3–7. Previously published in the *Chapbook*, q.v. (**217**). See *Twelve Idyls and Other Poems* (**28**) for notes on this poem.

(105)   A MISCELLANY OF POETRY 1920–1922

1922   *A Miscellany of Poetry* | 1920–1922 | *Edited by* | *William Kean Seymour* | *London* | *JOHN G. WILSON* | 350 *Oxford Street,* | *W.* 1

Format: 2 + x + 212 pages; Crown 8vo, $7\frac{1}{2} \times 5$ ins., all edges cut. Light blue boards, yellow cloth spine.

Publication Date: December, 1922.

Contribution: *In the Dunes* on pages 1–10. Previously published in *Voices*, q.v. (**617**). Later published in *Twelve Idyls and Other Poems*, q.v. (**28**) where notes on this poem will be found.

(106)   THE ENCYCLOPAEDIA BRITANNICA

1926   THE | ENCYCLOPÆDIA BRITANNICA | A DIC-TIONARY OF ARTS, | SCIENCES, LITERATURE | & GENERAL INFORMATION | [rule] | *THIR-TEENTH EDITION* | *Being Volumes One to Twenty-eight of the Latest Standard* | *Edition with the Three New Volumes Covering* | *Recent Years and the Index Volume* | [rule] | VOLUME 30 | THE THREE NEW VOLUMES | II | FABRE *to* OYAMA | [rule] | *LONDON* | THE ENCYCLOPÆDIA BRITANNICA COMPANY, LTD. | *NEW YORK* | THE ENCYCLOPÆDIA BRITAN-NICA, INC.

Format: xxviii + 1142 pages; Demy 4to, $11\frac{1}{2} \times 8\frac{1}{2}$ ins., all edges cut.

Maroon cloth, dark maroon leather spine and corners.

Publication Date: November, 1926.

Contribution: *Thomas Hardy* on page 316. This was volume 2 of the three additional volumes added to a reprint of the twelfth edition (1922). These volumes were issued in exactly the same form, probably on the same date, but with the title page:—

THE | ENCYCLOPÆDIA BRITANNICA | A DICTIONARY OF ARTS, | SCIENCES, LITERATURE | & GENERAL INFORMATION | [rule] | *The Three New Supplementary Volumes* | *constituting with the Volumes of the* | *Latest Standard Edition* | *THE THIRTEENTH EDITION* | [rule] | VOLUME II | FABRE *to* OYAMA | [rule] | *LONDON* | THE ENCYCLOPÆDIA BRITANNICA COMPANY, LTD. | *NEW YORK* | THE ENCYCLOPÆDIA BRITANNICA, INC.

The contribution was revised and expanded for the edition published in September, 1929 (volume 11, pages 192–193). Although the complete article was signed by L. A., it is probable he only contributed the second part: 'Three periods' and 'Poetry'. It was again slightly revised for the 1961 edition (same volume and pages), the second part now entitled 'Aspects of Hardy's genius' and the whole signed by L. A. and an anonymous contributor ('X').

(107)   GREAT NAMES

1926   GREAT NAMES | *Being an* Anthology *of* English | & American Literature *from* | CHAUCER *to* FRANCIS THOMPSON | *With* Introductions *by Various* | Hands & Drawings *by* J. F. HOR- | RABIN *after* Original Portraits | *The* Whole *Edited by* WALTER J. | TURNER *for* THE NONESUCH | PRESS & *here* First Published | *by* Special Arrangement | [publisher's emblem] | *Lincoln Mac Veagh* | NEW YORK: THE DIAL PRESS: MCMXXVI

Format: xii + 284 pages; Imperial 8vo, 10 × 7½ ins., all edges cut. Dark blue boards.

Publication Date: (mid-) December, 1926.

Two contributions: *Sir Thomas Browne* on pages 33–34, and *John Milton* on pages 38–39.

1927 BABEL | *A Dramatic Poem* | BY J. REDWOOD ANDER-
SON | LONDON: BOUVERIE HOUSE | ERNEST
BENN LIMITED | MCMXXVII

Format: 88 pages; Post 8vo, $7\frac{1}{4} \times 4\frac{3}{4}$ ins., all edges cut. Black cloth.

Publication Date: April (12?), 1927.

Contribution: *Preface* on pages 9–11; written at '37 Weetwood Lane, Far Headingley, Leeds'.

(109)   THE BOOK OF THE MICROCOSM

[1927] THE . BOOK . OF . THE | MICROCOSM | [row of
ornaments] | "AND . MICROCOSME . YS . A . WORD
. WYCH | CLERKYS . CALLE . THE . LESSE .
WORLDE." | [two ornaments] . EDITED BY . [two
ornaments] | DOROTHY . UNA . RATCLIFFE .
F.R.A.S., . F.R.G.S. | Scribe. M. Hopkins [all lettering
and ornaments in gilt and blue.]

Format: 120 pages; Post 4to, $9\frac{1}{2} \times 7\frac{1}{4}$ ins., all edges cut. Blue boards; blue cloth spine.

Publication Date: July, 1927 (edition undated).

Contribution: *White Love* on page 13. For notes on this poem see *Twelve Idyls and Other Poems* (28).

(110)   THE ILIAD OF HOMER

1928 THE | ILIAD | OF | HOMER | [swollen rule] | THE
FIRST TWELVE STAVES | TRANSLATED INTO
ENGLISH BY | MAURICE HEWLETT | [swollen rule]
| THE CRESSET PRESS LIMITED | *LONDON* |
MCMXXVIII

Format: $6 + xiv + 232$ pages; Imperial 8vo, $11\frac{1}{8} \times 7\frac{1}{2}$ ins., fore and lower edges uncut. Light brown buckram; white vellum spine.

Publication Date: January (26?), 1928.

Contribution: *Preface* on pages v–xiii. 'This edition is limited to 750 copies of which 725 are for sale in England and America. This copy is number . . .'.

(111)   THE SEA-MICROCOSM

[1929] *The* | SEA-MICROCOSM | *Edited by* | DOROTHY UNA RATCLIFFE | F.R.A.S. F.R.G.S. | *"You will never enjoy the world aright till the sea itself floweth in your veins,* | *till you are clothed with the heavens and crowned with the stars"*—TRAHERNE | *The Microcosm Office* | CITY CHAMBERS | LEEDS [all enclosed in a single line and ornamental border.]

Format: 100 pages; Post 4to, 9⅝ × 7⅛ ins., all edges cut. Blue boards; blue cloth spine.

Publication Date: July, 1929 (edition undated).

Contribution: *On Shipboard* on page 77. This is a poem of 20 lines, probably written for this book. It was later published as the first lines of the second act of *The Sale of Saint Thomas*, q.v. (**31**). In 1935 it was published in the anthology *Hoops of Steel* (printed for private circulation as 'a farewell supplement to the Microcosm') under the title 'On Shipboard (*to* you *via* "Sea-Swallow")'.

(112)   POEMS BY NICHOLAS NEKRASSOV

1929 POEMS BY | NICHOLAS NEKRASSOV | Translated by | JULIET M. SOSKICE | with an introduction by | LASCELLES ABERCROMBIE | ['World's Classics' series emblem] | OXFORD UNIVERSITY PRESS | LONDON: HUMPHREY MILFORD

Format: 2+xiv+196 pages (+16 pages of adverts); Foolscap 8vo, 5⅞ × 3½ ins., all edges cut. Dark blue cloth.

Publication Date: December, 1929.

Contribution: *Introduction* on pages vii–xiv. The book is number 340 in the 'World's Classics' series.

71

1930   FRIENDS IN SOLITUDE | by | PERCY WITHERS |
WITH AN INTRODUCTION BY LASCELLES
ABERCROMBIE | ['Travellers' Library' series emblem]
| LONDON | JONATHAN CAPE 30 BEDFORD
SQUARE

Format: $viii + 256$ pages; Post 8vo, $6\frac{3}{4} \times 4\frac{1}{2}$ ins., all edges cut. Buff cloth

Publication Date: March (28?), 1930.

Contribution: *Introduction* on pages v–x; written *c.* October 28, 1929.
The first edition of this book (1923) did not contain this introduction;
it first appeared in this 'Travellers' Library' edition.

(114)   GEORGE W. HARRIS

1931   GEORGE W. HARRIS | LONDON | NISBET & CO.
[1930] LTD.

Format: $xii + 24 + [180]$ (44 plates) pages; Royal 4to, $12\frac{1}{2} + 9\frac{3}{4}$ ins., all
edges cut.

Publication Date: January, 1931.

Contribution: *G. W. H.* on pages 12–18. 'This Edition is Limited to
425 Copies. Of which this is No. . . . .'.

(115)   HOMMAGE A RUPERT BROOKE

1931   HOMMAGE | A RUPERT BROOKE | ET A LA
POESIE | IMMORTELLE

Format: 40 pages; Foolscap 4to, $8\frac{1}{2} + 6\frac{3}{4}$ ins., all edges cut. Buff
wrappers.

Publication Date: June 15, 1931.

Untitled contribution on pages 19–20. 'Ce Livre Composé et Édité a
Athènes par les soins du bureau de la presse avec le gracieux concours
de M. M. G. Katisimbalis et M. Tombros est sorti des presses de
l'imprimerie "Hestia" le 15 Juin 1931.' A booklet issued after a cere-
mony to Rupert Brooke on April 5, 1931, at Skyros, Greece (where
Rupert Brooke is buried) when a statue was unveiled in his honour.
There are thirteen contributors to the booklet, French and English.

The small speech delivered by L. A. and printed here was given on behalf of the English Committee.

(116)　　　　　AN OUTLINE OF MODERN
　　　　　　　　　　　KNOWLEDGE

1931　EDITED BY DR. WILLIAM ROSE | AN OUTLINE OF | MODERN KNOWLEDGE | [list of eleven contributors on each title page, with their university posts, etc.] | ON [in red] | [list of thirteen general subjects on each title page, in red] | LONDON | VICTOR GOLLANCZ LTD. | 14 Henrietta Street Covent Garden | 1931

Format: xvi + 1104 pages; Demy 8vo, $8\frac{1}{2} \times 5\frac{3}{8}$ ins., all edges cut. Black cloth.

Publication Date: September 28, 1931.

Contribution: *Principles of Literary Criticism* on pages 859–907. It is subdivided into five parts: Introductory – The Art of Literature – Aristotle's 'Poetics' – After Aristotle – Conclusion. Possibly based on ten lectures given to Bedford College, London, on October 15, 22, 29, November 5, 12, 19, 26, December 3, 10, 17, 1930. It was published separately in 1932, q.v. (**33**).
　　There are two title pages facing each other; the layout, as above, is identical. Reprinted in October, 1931

(117)　　　　　　NEW ENGLISH POEMS

1931　NEW ENGLISH POEMS | *A MISCELLANY OF CONTEMPORARY VERSE | NEVER BEFORE PUBLISHED* | [short double rule] | The Collection Made | By LASCELLES ABERCROMBIE | LONDON | VICTOR GOLLANCZ LTD | 14 Henrietta Street Covent Garden

Format: Crown 8vo, $7\frac{1}{4} \times 4\frac{3}{4}$ ins.

Collation: 352 pages, consisting of:—
half-title, verso blank (pp. 1–2); title page, note on publication and imprint on verso (pp. 3–4); *Preface* signed by L. A. ('September 3rd., 1931') (pp. 5–8); *Note*, verso blank (pp. 9–10); *Contents* (pp. 11–17); page 18 blank; pages 19–352, text.

Binding: blue cloth; gilt lettering on spine; white end papers; all edges cut.

Signatures: Ap⁸ Bp–Xp⁸.

Publication Date: October, 1931.

He undertook to edit this at the beginning of July, 1931; all contributions to be in by August 24. There were 46 contributors, arranged alphabetically; L. A. contributed none of his own poetry.

The first and second impressions were published simultaneously; the first issue of 2,000 copies (priced 10s. 6d.), and the second issue of an unknown number (priced 6s.). They were both bound and produced in an identical manner.

(118) S. P. E. TRACT NO. XXXVI

1931 *S. P. E.* | *TRACT No. XXXVI* | COLLOQUIAL LANGUAGE IN LITERATURE | Lascelles Abercrombie | THE EXPANDED TENSES | Otto Jespersen | DISTANCE NO OBJECT | C. T. Onions | COMPRISE | H. W. Fowler | [publisher's emblem] | *At the Clarendon Press* | M DCCCCXXXI

Format: 24 pages (numbered *iv* + 517–535); Demy 8vo, 8¾ × 5½ ins., all edges uncut. Buff paper wrapper.

Publication Date: December 15, 1931.

Contribution: *Colloquial Language in Literature* on pages 517–523. This tract was in series vii of the Society of Pure English.

(119) REVALUATIONS

1931 REVALUATIONS | *STUDIES IN BIOGRAPHY* | *By* | LASCELLES ABERCROMBIE | LORD DAVID CECIL | G. K. CHESTERTON | G. D. H. COLE | STEPHEN GWYNN | JAMES LAVER | CAPTAIN LIDDELL HART | EDWARD MARJORIBANKS | NAOMI MITCHISON | T. EARLE WELBY || 1931 |

74

OXFORD UNIVERSITY PRESS | LONDON: HUMPHREY MILFORD

Format: xii+246 pages; Crown 8vo, 7½+5 ins., all edges uncut. Maroon cloth.

Publication Date: December (15?), 1931.

Contribution: *Tennyson* on pages 60–76. A lecture as read to the City Literary Institute, Holborn, London, on March 10, 1931.

(120)   HOMMAGE A RUPERT BROOKE
1887 1915

1931 HOMMAGE A | RUPERT BROOKE | 1887 1915 | Composé et présenté par | PAUL VANDERBORGHT | Poèmes de Rupert Brooke | traduits par | ROLAND HÉRELLE | 1931 | L'ÉGLANTINE | 20, rue de Lenglentier | BRUXELLES

Format: 224 pages; Post 4to, 9¾×7 ins., all edges uncut. Buff card wrapper.

Publication Date: 1931.

Contribution: *Rupert Brooke* on pages 137–143. The complete broadcast of April 22, 1930 (despite the fact the following note appeared under the text: 'conférence lue, le 23 avril 1930, au poste de T. S. F. de Londres, par le poète anglais Lascelles Abercrombie, professeur à l'Université de Londres'), translated into French. See Appendix I.

(121)   THE EIGHTEEN-SIXTIES

1932 THE | EIGHTEEN-SIXTIES | *ESSAYS* | by | Fellows of | the Royal Society of | Literature | Edited by | JOHN DRINKWATER | CAMBRIDGE | AT THE UNIVERSITY PRESS | 1932

Format: 2+x+284 pages; Demy 8vo, 8¾×5½ ins., fore and lower edges uncut. Brown cloth.

Publication Date: June (3?), 1932.

Contribution: *Sir Henry Taylor* on pages 1–19.

1932 TEN CONTEMPORARIES | NOTES TOWARD THEIR DEFINITIVE BIBLIOGRAPHY | by JOHN GAWSWORTH | with a Foreword by | VISCOUNT ESHER | [rule] | [ornament] | [rule] | and original essays by — | LASCELLES ABERCROMBIE | HERBERT E. PALMER | GEORGE EGERTON | SIR RONALD ROSS | STEPHEN HUDSON | EDITH SITWELL | WILFRID GIBSON | ROBERT NICHOLS | RHYS DAVIES | M. P. SHIEL | LONDON | ERNEST BENN LIMITED

Format: 224 pages; Post 8vo, $4\frac{3}{4} + 7\frac{1}{4}$ ins., all edges cut. Dark blue cloth.

Publication Date: June, 1932.

Contribution: *A Personal Note* on pages 17–21, followed by bibliographical notes of his principal books up to the end of 1931.

'John Gawsworth' is a pseudonym of Terence I. F. Armstrong.

(123) THE GREAT VICTORIANS

[1932] [rule] | THE GREAT | VICTORIANS | [quadruple rule] | IVOR NICHOLSON & WATSON, LTD. | 44 ESSEX STREET, STRAND, LONDON, W. C. | [double rule]

Format: xx + 556 pages; Demy 8vo, $8\frac{1}{2} \times 5\frac{1}{2}$ ins., all edges cut. Orange cloth.

Publication Date: August, 1932 (edition undated).

Contribution: *Robert Browning* on pages 81–93. This book was edited by H. J. and Hugh Massingham.

An edition was published by Penguin Books in November, 1937, in the 'Pelican Books' series (No. A. 11).

(124) SELECTED MODERN ENGLISH ESSAYS

1932 SELECTED | MODERN ENGLISH | ESSAYS | ['The World's Classics' series emblem] | *Second Series* | LONDON | OXFORD UNIVERSITY PRESS | HUMPHREY MILFORD

Format: 2 + x + 344 (+ 16 pages of advertisements) pages; Pott 8vo, $5\frac{3}{4} \times 3\frac{1}{2}$ ins., all edges cut. Dark blue cloth.

Publication Date: August, 1932.

Contribution: *A Plea for the Liberty of Interpreting* on pages 202–231. The book, edited by Humphrey S. Milford, is No. 406 in the 'World's Classics' series.

   This article was previously published in the *Proceedings of the British Academy*, q.v. (**586**), and was later published in *Aspects of Shakespeare*, q.v. (**126**).

(**125**)   THE LETTERS OF W. DIXON SCOTT

1932   THE LETTERS OF | W. DIXON SCOTT | *Edited by* | MARY McCROSSAN | *With a Preface by* | PROFESSOR LASCELLES ABERCROMBIE | LONDON | HERBERT JOSEPH 9 JOHN STREET ADELPHI

Format: 4+xx+296 pages; Demy 8vo, $8\frac{3}{4} \times 5\frac{1}{2}$ ins., fore and lower edges uncut. Blue cloth.

Publication Date: December, 1932.

Contribution: *Preface* on pages vii–xiii; written at '7a Stanley Gdns., London, W. 11'.

(**126**)   ASPECTS OF SHAKESPEARE

1933   ASPECTS | OF | SHAKESPEARE | Being | BRITISH ACADEMY LECTURES | By | L. ABERCROMBIE, E. K. CHAMBERS | H. GRANVILLE-BARKER, W. W. GREG | E. LEGOUIS, A. W. POLLARD | C. P. E. SPURGEON, A. THORNDIKE | AND J. D. WILSON | [ornament] | Oxford | AT THE CLARENDON PRESS | 1933

Format: viii+288 pages; Demy 8vo, $8\frac{7}{8} \times 5\frac{1}{2}$ ins., fore and lower edges uncut. Dark blue cloth.

Publication Date: February, 1933.

Contribution: *A Plea for the Liberty of Interpreting* on pages 227–254. This had previously been published in both the *Proceedings of the British Academy*, q.v. (**586**) and *Selected Modern English Essays*, q.v. (**124**).

1933 EDWARDIAN ENGLAND | A.D. 1901–1910 | A SERIES OF LECTURES DELIVERED AT KING'S COLLEGE, | UNIVERSITY OF LONDON, DURING THE SESSION 1932–3 | Edited by F. J. C. Hearnshaw, M.A., LL.D. | *Fellow of King's College and Professor of Medieval History in* | *the University of London* | LONDON | ERNEST BENN LIMITED

Format: 288 pages; Demy 8vo, $8\frac{1}{2} \times 5\frac{3}{8}$ ins., all edges cut. Dark blue cloth.

Publication Date: July, 1933.

Contribution: *Literature* (chapter VIII) on pages 185–203. A lecture as given to King's College, London, on November 30, 1932.

(128) ENGLISH CRITICAL ESSAYS

1934 ENGLISH | CRITICAL ESSAYS | *TWENTIETH*
[1933] *CENTURY* | SELECTED | WITH AN INTRODUC-TION | BY | PHYLLIS M. JONES | ['The World's Classics' series emblem] | *LONDON* | OXFORD UNIVERSITY PRESS | HUMPHREY MILFORD

Format: xvi+400 pages (+16 pages of advertisements); Pott 8vo, $6 \times 3\frac{1}{2}$ ins., all edges cut. Dark blue cloth.

Publication Date: January, 1934.

Contribution: *The Function of Poetry in the Drama* on pages 252–272. Previously published in *Poetry Review*, q.v. (**580**).
This book is No. 405 in the 'World's Classics' series.

(129) SOME APPRECIATIONS OF
WILLIAM MORRIS

1934 SOME APPRECIATIONS OF | WILLIAM MORRIS [two ornaments] | 24 MARCH 1934 [three ornaments] | EDITED BY GEO. ED. ROEBUCK | Issued by request of the Borough Council | Published by the Walthamstow |Antiquarian Society | January 1934

Format: 36 pages; Imperial 8vo, $10\frac{1}{2} \times 7\frac{1}{2}$ ins., all edges uncut. Cream wrapper.

Publication Date: January, 1934.

Untitled contribution on page 6. This booklet was issued upon the centenary of the birth of William Morris.

(130)   LADY PRECIOUS STREAM

1934   *Lady* | *PRECIOUS STREAM* | *AN OLD CHINESE PLAY DONE INTO* | *ENGLISH ACCORDING TO ITS* | *TRADITIONAL STYLE* | *by* S. I. HSIUNG | WITH A PREFACE BY | LASCELLES ABERCROM-BIE | 1934 | METHUEN & CO. LTD. LONDON | 36 ESSEX STREET W.C.

Format: (limited edition) xx+172 pages, Demy 8vo, $9\frac{1}{4} \times 5\frac{1}{2}$ ins., all edges uncut. Grey boards; white cloth spine. (Normal edition) xx+172 pages; Crown 8vo, $7\frac{1}{2} \times 5$ ins., fore and lower edges uncut. Dark blue cloth.

Publication Date: July 12, 1934.

Contribution: *Preface* on pages vii–x, written at 'Bedford College, March 1934'. The limited edition has the entry: 'This Edition, printed on hand made paper and signed by the author, is limited to 100 copies, of which this is No. . . .'.
There were many later editions.

(131)   CATALOGUE . . . OF WORKS BY
ERNEST PROCTOR

1936   CATALOGUE OF THE MEMORIAL | EXHIBITION OF WORKS BY | ERNEST PROCTOR, A.R.A. (1886–1935) | With an Appreciation by | Mr. LASCELLES ABERCROMBIE | ERNEST BROWN & PHILLIPS, Ltd. | (Directors: CECIL L. PHILLIPS, OLIVER F. BROWN) | THE LEICESTER GALLERIES | LEICES-TER SQUARE, LONDON | JANUARY, 1936 | EXHIBITION NO. 616

Format: 16 pages; Foolscap 8vo, $5\frac{5}{8} \times 4\frac{1}{4}$ ins., fore and lower edges uncut. Grey wrapper.

Publication Date: January, 1936.

Contribution: *Preface* on pages 5–8.

(132) THE COLLECTED POEMS OF JOHN DRINKWATER

1937 The Collected Poems | of John Drinkwater | Volume III
1923–1937 | Sidgwick and Jackson | Limited: London 1937

Format: xxiv + 344 pages; Demy 8vo, $8\frac{1}{8} \times 5\frac{5}{8}$ ins., fore and lower
edges uncut. Red buckram.

Publication Date: November, 1937.

Contribution: *John Drinkwater, 1882–1937: An Address given at the
Memorial Service at The Church of St Martin-in-the-Fields on April 2,
1937 by Lascelles Abercrombie* on pages v–xiii. Previously published in
English, q.v. (**247**).

(133) THE DICTIONARY OF NATIONAL BIOGRAPHY

1937 THE | DICTIONARY | of | NATIONAL BIOGRAPHY
| Founded in 1882 | by | GEORGE SMITH | [rule] |
1922–1930 | Edited by J. R. H. Weaver | [rule] | With an
Index covering the years 1901–1930 | in one alphabetical
series | OXFORD UNIVERSITY PRESS | LONDON:
HUMPHREY MILFORD

Format: 2 + xiv + 964 pages; Royal 8vo, $9\frac{1}{8} \times 6$ ins., all edges cut. Dark
blue cloth.

Publication Date: November, 1937.

Contribution: *Thomas Hardy* on pages 392–397; it was probably
written in 1933.

(134) LEEDS UNIVERSITY VERSE ANTHOLOGY

1949 LEEDS UNIVERSITY | *Verse Anthology* | *1924–1948* |
COMPILED BY | THE EDITORIAL STAFF OF THE
GRYPHON | [ornament] | 1949

Format: 80 pages; Demy 8vo, $8\frac{1}{2} \times 5\frac{1}{2}$ ins., all edges cut. Orange
boards.

Publication Date: April, 1949.

Contribution: *The Bazaar Address* on page 12; this title was not given to the poem by L. A., but by the compilers of the anthology. It was the first time this poem of 33 lines had been published. It was written in 1908 for a bazaar to be held at Grange-over-Sands, Lancashire, but was never used. When David Abercrombie was asked by the Gryphon to see if he could find an unpublished poem that could be included in this anthology, he approached Mrs. Jessie Vickers-Gaskell (the person for whom the poem was written) who consented to it being used. It is unlikely it had to be retrieved from a waste-paper basket, as the caption of the poem suggests. It was published here in facsimile form of a copy in L.A.'s hand.

'Ceremonial Ode' was also included in this anthology; for notes on this, see *Interludes and Poems* (1).

CONTRIBUTIONS TO
PERIODICALS AND NEWSPAPERS

The Academy
The Albany Review
The Athenaeum
The Bibelot
The Bibliophile's Almanack
The Blue Review
The Bookman
Boston Evening Transcript
The Bristol Playgoer
The British Institute of the University of Paris Bulletin
British Journal of Psychology
Bronte Society Publications: Transactions
Bulletin of the John Rylands Library
The Bulletin of the Sandon Studios Society
The Chapbook
The Classical Review
The Cornhill Magazine
Daily Express
Daily Herald
Daily News
Daily News and Leader
English
The English Review
The Fortnightly
The Highway
The Independent Review
The Listener
Littell's Living Age
The Liverpool Chapbook
The Liverpool Courier
The Liverpool Echo
Liverpool Post and Mercury
Manchester City News
Manchester Guardian
The Microcosm
The Modern Language Review
Morning Post
The Nation
The Nation and the Athenæum
New Numbers
The New Statesman and Nation
The New Weekly
Nineteenth Century and After
The Observer
The Parents' Review
Poetry and Drama

The Poetry Review
The Proceedings of the British Academy
Proceedings of the Leeds Philosophical and Literary Society
Proceedings of the Royal Institution
The Quarterly Review
The ReandeaN News Sheet
The Review of English Studies
Rhythm
Science Progress
Theatre Arts Magazine
The Times
The Times Educational Supplement
The Times Literary Supplement
The Town Planning Review
The Trawl
The Vineyard
Voices
The Year's Work in English Studies
[Untraced periodical]

THE ACADEMY

(201) 1908 February 15 (Vol. LXXIV, No. 1867)

Letter (p. 472): 'Cockney Rhymes', dated February 9 [1908].

(202) 1908 May 23 (Vol. LXXIV, No. 1881)

Letter (p. 816): 'The Bluecoat Hospital At Liverpool' dated May 20, 1908.

THE ALBANY REVIEW

(203) 1908 July (Vol. III, No. 16)

Prose dialogue (pp. 417–428): *Famine and Pestilence.*

Reprinted in *Littell's Living Age*, q.v. **(259)**; for notes on this, see *Speculative Dialogues* **(12)**.

THE ATHENAEUM

(204) 1919 June 6 (No. 4649)

Letter (p. 438): 'Modern Poetry and Modern Society'.

THE BIBELOT

(205) 1910 February (Vol. XVI, No. 2)

Book review (pp. 65–72): *The Riding to Lithend,* by Gordon Bottomley.

Reprinted from the *Liverpool Courier,* q.v. **(338)**.

THE BIBLIOPHILE'S ALMANACK

(206) [1927] [Annual for 1928]

Poetic drama (pp. 43–61): *Bothwell's End: Fragment of an Unfinisht Play.*

A poetic drama of three scenes, with the number of lines: scene I, 114; II, 121; III, 52. It is not known when it was written, but probably between 1910 and 1914. It was never published again.

THE BLUE REVIEW

(207) 1913 June (Vol. I, No. II)

Article (pp. 117–122): *Poetry.*

This considers the previous month's poetry by expanding reviews.

THE BOOKMAN

(208) 1930 December (Vol. LXXIX)

Article (pp. 166–167): *Robert Bridges: Technique and 'The Testament of Beauty'.*

An article under the main heading 'A Century of Laureates'.

BOSTON EVENING TRANSCRIPT

(209)* 1914 July 8

Book review: *North of Boston,* by Robert Frost.

Excerpts of the review in the *Nation,* q.v. **(559)**.

THE BRISTOL PLAYGOER

(210) 1914 December (No. 17)

Article (pp. 5–8): *War and the Drama* [part 1].

(211) 1915 January (No. 18)

Article (pp. 11–14): *War and the Drama* [part 2].

This article, divided between the two issues, was probably 'commissioned' by the Bristol Playgoers Club after L. A. had lectured to them in Bristol, about October 31, 1914.

THE BRITISH INSTITUTE OF THE UNIVERSITY OF PARIS BULLETIN

(212)* 1938 January (No. 3)

Article (pp. 7–13): *Extracts from the Lecture upon Ben Jonson.*

This lecture, entitled 'Ben Jonson: Poet and Critic', was given in the Amphitheatre Richelieu, Paris, under the auspices of the Institute and Association France-Grande-Bretagne, on December 1, 1937.

BRITISH JOURNAL OF PSYCHOLOGY

(213) 1923 July (Vol. XIV [General Section], Part 1)

Article (pp. 68–77): *Communication versus Expression in Art.*

This was a lecture as read to the Aesthetics Section of the British Psychological Society at Bedford College, London, on January 29, 1923. It was issued separately from the *Journal* in a twelve page pamphlet.

BRONTE SOCIETY PUBLICATIONS: TRANSACTIONS

(214) 1924 [Annual] (Vol. VI, Part XXXIV)

Article (pp. 179–200): *The Brontës Today.*

'An address . . . delivered at the Annual Meeting of the Bront Society, held at Bradford, March 8th, 1924.'

BULLETIN OF THE JOHN RYLANDS LIBRARY

(215) 1935 January (Vol. 19, No. 1)

Article (pp. 216–229): *Herford and International Literature.*

This was the fourth Herford Memorial Lecture as delivered to the Manchester Dante Society in the University of Manchester on October 3, 1934. Issued separately from the *Bulletin* in a sixteen page pamphlet.

THE BULLETIN OF THE SANDON STUDIOS SOCIETY

216) 1913 August (No. 6)

Tale (pp. [9–11]): *Devil's Man.*

Originally appeared in the *Trawl*, q.v. (**613**).

THE CHAPBOOK

217) 1922 February (No. 25)

Poem (pp. 16–22): *Ryton Firs (A Fragment).*

For notes on this, see *Twelve Idyls* (**28**).

(218) 1923 February (No. 34)

Dramatic poem (pp. 2–15): *Ham and Eggs.*

For notes, see *Twelve Idyls* (**28**).

THE CLASSICAL REVIEW

219) 1927 December (Vol. XLI, No. 6)

Book review (pp. 235–237): *What is Rhythm? An Essay,* by E. A. Sonnenschein.

THE CORNHILL MAGAZINE

220) 1935 February (Vol. 151, No. 902)

Tale (pp. 206–212): *Marriage of True Minds.*

Proofs corrected in November, 1934.

DAILY EXPRESS

(221) 1928 July 5 (No. 8794)

Poem (p. 10): *The Stream's Song.*

For notes on this, see *Twelve Idyls* (**28**).

(222) 1919 June 4 (No. 1049 [56, new series])

Article (p. 8): *Thomas Hardy.*

Written May 26 and 27, 1919.

DAILY NEWS

All contributions by L. A. to this paper are book reviews, all being signed in full. It is possible he contributed some leading articles, but none can be traced. He probably started contributing just before January 26, 1910, but nothing has been traced until the first signed review of February 4. The signing of this caused him considerable trouble with the *Liverpool Courier,* who did not allow their permanent staff to contribute to other papers. L. A. was brought up in front of the *Courier* directors, and was 'pulled over the coals'. However, he remained on the staff of the *Courier* while still contributing to the *Daily News* and the *Manchester Guardian* (it appears that contributing to the *Nation* was not prevented or even frowned up on by the *Courier*).

(223) 1910 February 4 (No. 19937)

(p. 3): *England and Other Poems,* by Laurence Binyon; *Baudelaire: The Flower of Evil,* translated by Cyril Scott; *The Poems of Sappho,* translated by Percy Osborn.

(224) 1910 April 19 (No. 20000)

(p. 4): *The 'Iphigenia In Tauris' of Euripides,* translated by Gilbert Murray.

(225) 1910 May 16 (No. 20023)

(p. 3): *Ambergris,* a selection from the poems of Aleister Crowley; *Daily Bread. Book I. The House of Candles. Book II. The Garret,* by Wilfrid Wilson Gibson.

(226) 1910 June 29 (No. 20061)

(p. 4): *Gathered Leaves from the Prose of Mary E. Coleridge*, with a memoir by Edith Sichel.

(227) 1910 August 12 (No. 20099)

(p. 3): *Walter Headlam: His Letters and Poems*, with a memoir by Cecil Headlam.

(228) 1910 August 25 (No. 20110)

(p. 3): *The Laureate of Pessimism: A Sketch of the Life and Character of James Thomson ('B.V.')*, by Bertram Dobell.

(229) 1910 September 19 (No. 20131)

(p. 3): *Rest Harrow: A Comedy of Resolution*, by Maurice Hewlett.

(230) 1910 October 5 (No. 20145)

(p. 4): *Heinrich Heine's Memoirs*, edited by Gustav Karpeles.

(231) 1910 December 14 (No. 20205)

(p. 5): *Stefan George: Selection from His Works*, translated by Cyril Scott; *Le Roi D'Ys, and Other Poems*, by Lewis Spence; *Arion of Lesbos and Other Poems*, by Kitty Balbernie.

(232) 1911 January 16 (No. 20233)

(p. 3): *The Origin of Tragedy, with Special Reference to the Greek Tragedies*, by William Ridgeway.

(233) 1911 February 16 (No. 20260)

(p. 3): *A Collection of Ballads*, edited by Andrew Lang; *Sir Walter Scott and the Border Minstrelsy*, by Andrew Lang.

(234) 1911 March 17 (No. 20285)

(p. 3): *A Book of Verse by Living Women*, with an introduction by Lady Margaret Sackville; *Eyes of Youth*, a book of verse, with a forward by Gilbert K. Chesterton.

(235) 1911 April 18 (No. 20312)

(p. 6): *From the East and From the West*, by T. C. Lewis; *Sanctuary and Other Poems*, by R. G. T. Coventry; *Songs of a Shopman*, by Arthur Hickmott.

(236) 1911 May 10 (No. 20331)
(p. 4): *Lysistrata. A Modern Paraphrase from the Greek of Aristophanes*, by Laurence Housman; *Medea and Circe, and other Poems*, by Arthur K. Sabin.

(237) 1911 June 30 (No. 20375)

(p. 4): *Week-Day Poems*, by Hugh Owen.

(238) 1911 August 14 (No. 20413)

(p. 7): *The Little Dream*, by John Galsworthy.

(239) 1911 September 11 (No. 20437)

(p. 7): *The Accuser*; *Tristan de Leonois*; *A Messiah*; *The Tragedy of Pardon*; *Diane*, all by the author of *Borgia* [Michael Field]; *Desiderio*, by Maurice Baring.

(240) 1912 January 23 (No. 20552)

(p. 4): *English Songs of Italian Freedom*, edited by George Macaulay Trevelyan; *Cophetua: A Play In One Act*, by John Drinkwater.

(241) 1912 February 27 (No. 20582)

(p. 3): *Psyche*, by Francis Coutts; *Before Dawn: Poems and Impressions*, by Harold Monro.

DAILY NEWS AND LEADER

The first issue under this name was May 13, 1912; numerically continuous with the *Daily News*.

(242) 1912 June 21 (No. 20681)

(p. 8): *A Tragedy in Stone and Other Papers*, by Lord Redesdale.

(243) 1912 July 22 (No. 20707)

(p. 8): *Letters of William Cowper*, chosen and edited with a memoir by J. G. Frazer.

(244) 1912 August 26 (No. 20737)

(p. 6): *The Iscariot*, by Eden Phillpotts; *Hail Mary*, by Aleister Crowley; *Poems*, by Gerald Gould.

(245) 1912 November 4 (No. 20797)

(p. 8): *The Poetical Works of George Meredith*, with some notes by G. M. Trevelyan.

(246) 1913 March 18 (No. 20911)

(p. 4): *Charles Dickens*, by Algernon Charles Swinburne.

ENGLISH

(247) 1937 [April] (Vol. 1, No. 5)

Article (pp. 384–389): *John Drinkwater.*

'An address given at the Memorial Service at the Church of St. Martin-in-the-Fields, 2 April, 1937.' Later published in the *Collected Poems of John Drinkwater*, q.v. (**132**).

(248) 1937 [June] (Vol. 1, No. 6)

Book review (pp. 562–563): *1904–1936: Poems*, by Lord Gorell.

THE ENGLISH REVIEW

(249) 1912 June (Vol. XI)

Poem (pp. 339–342): *[Ode To] Marie Spiridonova.*

This is a poem of 144 lines, begun on June 24, 1908. When it was finished is not known, nor are there any other details. It was never published again.

(250) 1913 February (Vol. XIII)

Article (pp. 418–429): *Phonetics and Poetry.*

THE FORTNIGHTLY

(251) 1936 January (Vol. CXXXIX, [No. 1])

Book review (pp. 115–116): *The Works of Thomas Lovell Beddoes,* and *The Browning Box,* edited and introduced by H. W. Donner; *Thomas Lovell Beddoes,* by H. W. Donner.

THE HIGHWAY

(252) 1923 March (Vol. XV, No. 7)

Book review (pp. 102–103): *The Oresteia of Aeschylus,* translated by R. C. Trevelyan.

(253) 1930 October (Vol. XXIII, [No. 2])

Article (pp. 6–7): '*The Finest Passage in the Bible*'.

THE INDEPENDENT REVIEW

(254) 1907 March (Vol. XII, No. 42)

Dramatic poem (pp. 292–310): *Blind.*

For notes on this poem, see *Interludes and Poems* (**1**).

THE LISTENER

(255) 1930 April 30 (Vol. III, No. 68)

Article (pp. 775–776): *After Fifteen Years – An Appreciation of Rupert Brooke.*

This was reduced from a broadcast given by the B.B.C. on April 22, 1930 (see Appendix I).

(256) 1931 November 18 (Vol. VI, No. 149)

Book review (supplement, p. vii): *Collected Poems,* by Laurence Binyon.

(257) 1934 May 9 (Vol. XI, No. 287)

Book review (p. 810): *Collected Essays and Papers of Robert Bridges; Nos. XI–XV.*

(258) 1934 August 15 (Vol. XII, No. 292)

Poem (p. 300): *To Sir Walford Davies (Spoken at the Gregynog Festival of Music).*

For notes on this poem, see *To Sir Walford Davies* (**39**).

LITTELL'S LIVING AGE

(259)★ 1908 September 19 (Vol. 258)

Prose dialogue (pp. 745–751): *Famine and Pestilence.*

Reprinted from the *Albany Review*, q.v. (**203**); for notes, see *Speculative Dialogues* (**12**).

(260)★ 1916 January 1 (Vol. 288)

Article (pp. 3–15): *The War and the Poets.*

Reprinted from the *Quarterly Review*, q.v. (**589**).

(261)★ 1926 January 23 (Vol. 328)

Article (pp. 207–209): *Perfect Moments.*

Reprinted from the *Manchester Guardian*, q.v. (**540**).

THE LIVERPOOL CHAPBOOK

This periodical was apparently edited by L. A. and John Pride, lasting one issue only. The foreword on pages 1–2, signed by 'The Editor', is divided into four parts by asterisks; it is possible L. A. contributed the second and third parts, but this cannot be confirmed.

(262) 1920 November (No. 1)

Poem (p. 2): *Armistice Day.*

Later published as the second stanza of 'Inscriptions' in *Twelve Idyls*, q.v. (**28**).

He began contributing occasional material to this paper sometime towards the end of January, 1908, but as nothing was signed and no mention was made in letters, no contributions have been traced until August, 1908 when he joined the staff as a leader writer and book reviewer. '. . . They offered me £2. 10. a week, and seem rather to want me. The work is about two leaders a week, book-reviewing and some hack-work, as obituary notices of nobs', but no political stuff and no journalistic drudgery of the base type', he said in a letter of August 1, 1908. It is uncertain how he secured the job, but it is likely that Walter Dixon Scott, who was then writing leaders and reviews for the paper, and was a great friend of L. A., helped him get an interview with Robert Hield, the editor. He began work on August 2, 1908.

It is extremely difficult to ascertain the leading articles that were contributed by L. A. (they were, of course, unsigned), for although his letters help to point to the majority of dates of the papers, there were usually three or four leaders per issue, only one being by L. A. The method used here is to eliminate those leaders on subjects which one can say with almost total certainty he would not have written. Those listed are from each issue to which it is known he contributed, and are qualified by 'probably' and 'possibly'. Those not qualified he certainly wrote. Of the reviews, only definite and probable have been included. The reviews noted here were usually signed by initials, but some were either signed in full or unsigned. All articles other than leaders were signed in full. Although he probably contributed many music concert reviews, a search of letters and original newspapers revealed only a few.

(**263**) 1908 August 7 (No. 19753)

> Leader (p. 4): *The Way of the Poet.*

> This was his first leader.

(**264**) 1908 August 8 (No. 19754)

> Leader (p. 4): possibly *Intending Passengers and Moving Trams.*

(265) 1908 August 11 (No. 19756)

Leader (p. 4): probably *Airships and Landscape.*

Written August 9.

(266) 1908 August 13 (No. 19758)

Leader (p. 4): probably *English Versus African Crockery.*

An article on Negro Pottery was written for the *Nation*, but refused by them in August, 1908. It is safe to assume this is probably the article.

(267) 1908 August 14 (No. 19759)

Leader (p. 4): probably *Climate and Clothes.*

Book review (p. 8): probably *The Camper's Handbook*, by T. H. Holding.

(268) 1908 August 18 (No. 19762)

Leader (p. 4): probably *The Significance of the Conjuror.*

(269) 1908 August 19 (No. 19763)

Leader (p. 6): *The Arrested Leprechaun.*

Written August 18.

(270) 1908 August 20 (No. 19764)

Leader (p. 6): probably *The Defilement of English.*

Written August 19.

(271) 1908 August 21 (No. 19765)

Leader (p. 6): probably *Slum Usurers.*

Book review (p. 9): *Lord Kelvin, an Account of his Scientific Life and Work*, by Prof. Andrew Gray. Also *Johnson on Shakespeare: Essays and Notes*, edited by Walter Raleigh.

(272) 1908 August 25 (No. 19768)

Leader (p. 4): *Problem of the Dollar.*

Written August 22.

(273) 1908 August 26 (No. 19769)

Leader (p. 4): *West and East*

Written August 23.

(274) 1908 August 28 (No. 19771)

Leader (p. 6): possibly '*Tyburn Tree*'.

Book review (p. 10): *The Red Lily*; *Mother of Pearl*; and *The Garden of Epicurus*, all by Anatole France.

(275) 1908 September 4 (No. 19777)

Leader (p. 6): probably *An Opening for Trade.*

Book review (p. 10): *Selections from Erasmus, Principally from his Epistles*, by P. S. Allen.

(276) 1908 September 9 (No. 19781)

Leader (p. 7): *The Faust Legend on the Stage.*

Written September 7.

(277) 1908 September 11 (No. 19783)

Leader (p. 6): *The Cotton Dispute.*

Book review (p. 10): *Concerning Lafcadio Hearn*, by George M. Gould.

(278) 1908 September 14 (No. 19785)

Leader (p. 6): *The Persistance of Poetry.*

(279) 1908 September 16 (No. 19787)

Obituary (p. 7): *Professor's Sad End: Death of Mr. Churton Collins. A Loss to Literature.*

Written September 15.

(280) 1908 September 18 (No. 19789)

Leader (p. 6): probably *The Johnson Celebrations.*

Book review (p. 10): probably *The Life of Tolstoy: First Fifty Years,* by Aylmer Maude.

(281) 1908 September 21 (No. 19791)

Leader (p. 6): *The Drama in Liverpool.*

Probably written September 19.

(282) 1908 September 25 (No. 19795)

Leader (p. 6): probably *Popularity and Art.*

Book review (p. 10): *Selected Poems of Francis Thompson,* with a note by Wilfred Meynell.

(283) 1908 September 29 (No. 19798)

Leader (p. 6): probably *Egoism.*

(284) 1908 September 30 (No. 19799)

Leader (p. 7): probably *The Call of the Country.*

(285) 1908 October 1 (No. 19800)

Leader (p. 6): probably *Cat's Day.*

(286) 1908 October 2 (No. 19801)

Leader (p. 6): *Blanco-White.*

Book review (p. 9): *The Brontes: Life and Letters,* by Clement Shorter. Also probably *Herculaneum: Past, Present and Future,* by Charles Waldstein and Leonard Shoobridge. Also *Peter Pink-Eye*; *The Magic Wand*; *The Princess and the Dragon,* all by S. H. Hamer. And *John the Baptist: a play,* by Hermann Sudermann.

(287) 1908 October 3 (No. 19802)

Leader (p. 7): possibly *Foolish Obstinacy.*

(288) 1908 October 5 (No. 19804)

Book review (p. 9): probably *The Life of Henry Irving*, by Austin Brereton.

(289) 1908 October 9 (No. 19807)

Leader (p. 6): probably *The Psychology of Compromise*.

Book review (p. 9): *The Sword of Welleran, and other Stories*, by Lord Dunsany.

(290) 1908 October 14 (No. 19811)

Leader (p. 7): probably *Shakespeare's Impartiality*.

(291) 1908 October 16 (No. 19813)

Leader (p. 6): probably *Exposure and Vindication*.

Book review (p. 10): *Chaucer and His England*, by G. G. Coulton.

(292) 1908 October 19 (No. 19815)

Leader (p. 6): probably *The Untrustworthiness of History*.

(293) 1908 October 22 (No. 19818)

Book review (p. 9): *The Life of James McNeill Whistler*, by E. R. and J. Pennell.

Written October 20.

(294) 1908 October 23 (No. 19819)

Leader (p. 6): probably *The Perfect City*.

Book review (p. 10): *Richard Strauss*, by Ernest Newman.

(295) 1908 October 30 (No. 19825)

Leader (p. 6): *Too Much Literature?*

Concert review: Nicholls' Chamber Concert.

[Not examined; this is probably in the first edition only.]

(296) 1908 October 31 (No. 19826)

Leader (p. 6): *The Happy Ending.*

Written October 30.

(297) 1908 November 2 (No. 19827)

Leader (p. 6): probably *Our Book Exhibition.*

(298) 1908 November 3 (No. 19828)

Concert review (p. 11): *Liverpool Symphony Orchestra: Third Concert.*

(299) 1908 November 6 (No. 19831)

Leader (p. 6): probably *Fire-Worship.*

(300) 1908 November 16 (No. 19839)

Leader (p. 6): *The Man with the Message.*

Written in collaboration with Robert Hield on November 15.

(301) 1908 November 17 (No. 19840)

Leader (p. 6): probably *The Chinese Enigma.*

(302) 1908 November 19 (No. 19842)

Leader (p. 7): *Banners.*

(303) 1908 November 20 (No. 19843)

Leader (p. 6): *The Teaching of Art.*

Book review (p. 10): *The Philosophy of Friedrich Nietzsche,* by Henry L. Mencken. Also *Characters,* by Samuel Butler.

(304) 1908 November 23 (No. 19845)

Concert review (p. 5): *The Music of Sibelius: Third Symphony at the Orchestral Concert.*

Probably written November 21.

Leader (p. 6): *A Word on Spelling Reform.*

Written November 22.

(305) 1908 November 27 (No. 19849)

Leader (p. 6): *Mountain Influences.*

(306) 1908 November 28 (No. 19850)

Book review (p. 8): *London Visions,* by Laurence Binyon.

(307) 1908 December 1 (No. 19852)

Leader (pp. 6–7): probably *The Control of Pleasures*

Written November 28 or 29.

(308) 1908 December 4 (No. 19855)

Leader (p. 7): probably *Box-Office Criticism.*

Book review (p. 9): probably *The Wind in the Willows,* by Kenneth Grahame.

(309) 1908 December 8 (No. 19858)

Poem (p. 5): *The Charge of the Knights' Brigade.*

This unsigned poem of 40 lines was written in collaboration with Robert Hield, editor of the *Courier,* on December 7 as a parody of Tennyson's 'Charge of the Light Brigade', and was included in the daily feature 'The Passing Hour'. Immediately under the title, and before the text of the poem, was the note: 'At the Albert Hall Suffragist meeting on Saturday [December 5] nearly a hundred "gentlemen volunteers" acted as stewards and "chuckers out"'.

Article (p. 9): *Milton and the Superman.*

(310) 1908 December 10 (No. 19860)

Leader (p. 6): *The Ideal Poet.*

(311) 1908 December 11 (No. 19861)

Leader (p. 6): probably *New Use for Beggars.*

(312) 1908 December 14 (No. 19863)

Leader (p. 7): *Music in Schools.*

(313) 1908 December 18 (No. 19867)

Leader (p. 6): possibly *The Prosperity of the Port.*

Book review (p. 9): probably *Faust,* freely adapted from Goethe's dramatic poem by Stephen Phillips and J. Comyns Carr.

(314) 1908 December 25 (No. 19873)

Leader (p. 4): *Christmas.*

(315) 1908 December 26 (No. 19874)

Leader (p. 4): possibly *A Green Christmas.*

From this point the reference to leading articles in letters by L. A. were so scarce, that although he almost certainly contributed a great many more, very few can be traced. Before, it had been deemed satisfactory to assume that he had contributed a leader every Friday, and probably at least one other a week. As it is not known when this arrangement was discontinued, it seems appropriate to list only the definite leaders from this point on.

(316) 1909 January 1 (No. 19879)

Book review (p. 8): *Poems by John Clare.*

(317) 1909 January 8 (No. 19885)

Book review (p. 10): *The Immortal Hour,* by Fiona Macleod.

(318) 1909 January 16 (No. 19892)

Leader (p. 7): *The Disadvantage of Justice.*

(319) 1909 January 19 (No. 19894)

Article (p. 9): *Edgar Allen Poe. A Master of Form.*

(320) 1909 January 22 (No. 19897)

> Book review (p. 9): *Frederick Nietzsche: His Life and Work*, by M. A. Mugge; *Who Is To Be Master of the World*, by A. M. Ludovici.

(321) 1909 February 12 (No. 19915)

> Book review (p. 9): *Aspects of Modern Opera*, by Lawrence Gilman.

(322) 1909 March 12 (No. 19939)

> Book review (p. 9): *Psyche's Task*, by J. G. Frazer.

(323) 1909 March 19 (No. 19945)

> Book review (p. 10): *The Cambridge History of English Literature (Vol. III)*, edited by A. W. Ward and A. R. Waller.

(324) 1909 April 2 (No. 19957)

> Book review (p. 9): *Shelley*, by Francis Thompson.

(325) 1909 April 24 (No. 19976)

> Leader (p. 6): *Shakespeare Day.*

(326) 1909 May 14 (No. 19993)

> Book review (p. 10): *A Brief Account of Gypsy History, Persecutions, Character, and Customs, with Examples of Genuine Gypsy Melodies*, compiled by Bob Skot.

(327) 1909 June 4 (No. 20011)

> Book review (p. 9): *Artemision: Idylls and Songs*, by Maurice Hewlett.

(328) 1909 June 11 (No. 20017)

> Book review (p. 9): *Scandinavian Britain*, by W. G. Collingwood.

(329) 1909 June 25 (No. 20029)

Book review (p. 9): *Oxford Lectures on Poetry*, by A. C. Bradley.

(330) 1909 July 9 (No. 20041)

Book review (p. 9): *Mendel's Principles of Heredity*, by Prof. W. Bateson.

(331) 1909 July 23 (No. 20053)

Book review (p. 10): *The Complete Works of Friedrich Nietzsche*.

(332) 1909 August 13 (No. 20071)

Book review (p. 10): *Sonnets*, by Lord Alfred Douglas.

(333) 1909 August 20 (No. 20077)

Book review (p. 9): *Egoists: A Book of Supermen*, by James Huneker.

(334) 1909 August 27 (No. 20083)

Book review (p. 9): *Fleet Street and Other Poems*, by John Davidson.

(335) 1909 September 3 (No. 20089)

Book review (p. 9): *George Bernard Shaw*, by Gilbert K. Chesterton.

(336) 1909 September 17 (No. 20101)

Book review (p. 9): *The Cliffs*, by Charles M. Doughty.

(337) 1909 September 29 (No. 20111)

Leader (p. 7): *The Shakespeare League.*

(338) 1909 October 1 (No. 20113)

Book review (p. 9): *Riding To Lithend,* by Gordon Bottomley.

Reprinted in the *Bibelot,* q.v. **(205)**.

(339) 1909 October 4 (No. 20115)

Leader (p. 6): *Shakespeare as Financier.*

(340) 1909 October 8 (No. 20119)

Book review (p. 9): probably *Actions and Reactions,* by Rudyard Kipling.

(341) 1909 October 22 (No. 20131)

Leader (p. 6): *A Liverpool Poet.*

Book review (p. 9): *The Tragedy of Nan, and Other Plays,* by John Masefield.

(342) 1909 November 12 (No. 20149)

Book review (p. 9): *Tremendous Trifles,* by G. K. Chesterton.

(343) 1909 November 19 (No. 20155)

Book review (p. 9): *The Life of Joan of Arc,* by Anatole France.

(344) 1909 December 17 (No. 20179)

Book review (p. 9): *The Complete Works of Friedrich Nietzsche,* edited by Dr. Oscar Levy. Also *Legends and Stories of Italy for Children,* by Amy Steedman.

(345) 1909 December 31 (No. 20191)

Book review (p. 8): *Cesar Frank,* by Vincent d'Indy.

In January, 1910, this paper was taken over by a new board of directors (the editorship remained with Robert Hield), and L. A. was given more special articles to write and probably considerably less leader writing. The first special under this new 'regime' was on January 27, 1910.

In April, 1910, L. A. left the staff and moved to Much Marcle, Herefordshire, probably contributing only very occasionally from then on.

(**346**) 1910 January 21 (No. 20209)

Book review (p. 9): *The Great French Revolution, 1789–1793*, by P. A. Kropotkin.

(**347**) 1910 January 27 (No. 20214)

Article (p. 9): *Sappho, the Inventor of Love. Recently Discovered Poems.*

Written January 25.

(**348**) 1910 February 4 (No. 20221)

Article (p. 9): *A Marriage of East and West. Anglo Japanese Poetry.*

Written February 3.

(**349**) 1910 February 11 (No. 20227)

Article (p. 9): *Egypt Today. Two Spirits in Conflict.*

Written February 7.

(**350**) 1910 March 18 (No. 20257)

Book review (p. 9): *A History of English Poetry*, by W. J. Courthope.

(**351**) 1910 April 15 (No. 20281)

Article (p. 9): *The Artist's Mind. Painters and Their Art.*

(**352**) 1910 July 30 (No. 20372)

Article (p. 9): *Adventures Afoot. The Glamour of Wales.*

(**353**) 1910 August 5 (No. 20377)

Book review (p. 9): *The Deeds of Beowulf*, done into modern prose by John Earle.

(354) 1910 September 23 (No. 20419)

Book review (p. 9): *An Affair of Dishonour*, by William De Morgan.

(355) 1910 October 14 (No. 20437)

Book review (p. 9): *The Cambridge History of English Literature*, edited by A. W. Ward and A. R. Waller.

(356) 1910 November 25 (No. 20473)

Book review (p. 9): *Edgar Allen Poe. A Critical Study*, by Arthur Ransome.

(357) 1910 December 16 (No. 20491)

Book review (p. 9): *The Origin of Tragedy*, by William Ridgeway.

(358) 1911 February 17 (No. 20545)

Book review (p. 9): *The Joyful Wisdom. The Will To Power. Vol. II*, by Friedrich Nietzsche; *The Gospel of Superman*, by Henri Lichtenberger.

(359) 1911 March 31 (No. 20581)

Book review (p. 9): *The Patrician*, by John Galsworthy; *The New Machiavelli*, by H. G. Wells.

(360) 1911 April 8 (No. 20588)

Book review (p. 9): *Selections from Ancient Irish Poetry*, translated by Kuno Meyer.

(361) 1911 May 26 (No. 20629)

Book review (p. 9): *Shakespeare Bibliography*, by William Jaggard.

(362) 1911 June 5 (No. 20637)

Book review (p. 11): *The Abuse of the Singing and Speaking Voice*, by E. J. Moure and A. Bourger; *The Brain and the Voice in Speech and Song*, by F. W. Mott.

(363) 1911 July 7 (No. 20665)

Book review (p. 9): *Essays on Two Moderns*, by W. H. Salter; *Greek Love Songs and Epigrams*, translated by G. A. Pott.

(364) 1911 July 21 (No. 20677)

Book review (p. 9): *The Revolutions of Civilisation*, by W. M. Flinders Petrie.

(365) 1911 September 2 (No. 20714)

Book review (p. 9): *Biographia Epistolaris: Being the Biographical Supplement of Coleridge's 'Biographia Literaria'*, edited by A. Turnbull.

(366) 1911 October 13 (No. 20749)

Book review (p. 9): *Family Letters of Richard Wagner*, translated etc. by William Ashton Ellis.

(367)* 1911 (November ?)

Book review (untraced): *The Mastery of Life*, by G. T. Wrench.

(368) 1911 December 15 (No. 20803)

Book review (p. 9): *The Invaded Solitude*, by Magdalen Rawlins.

(369) 1912 March 1 (No. 20869)

Book review (p. 9): *The Complete Works of Friedrich Nietzsche*, edited by Dr. Oscar Levy.

(370) 1912 May 31 (No. 20947)

Book review (p. 9): *William James*, by Emile Boutroux; *Hewin Bergson*, by H. Wildon Carr; *Eucken and Bergson: Their Significance for Christian Thought*, by F. Hermann; *Critical Exposition of Bergson's Philosophy*, by J. McKellar Stewart; *Life's*

Basis and Life's Ideal, by Rudolph Eucken; *The Principles of Individuality and Value*, by Bernard Bosanquet; *Hegel's Charlatanism Exposed*, by M. Kelly.

(371) 1912 June 14 (No. 20959)

Book review (p. 9): *Mariamne*, by T. Sturge Moore; *Sicilian Idyll and Judith*, by T. Sturge Moore.

(372) 1912 June 15 (No. 20960)

Book review (p. 9): *Allegory of Othello*, by Charles Creighton.

THE LIVERPOOL ECHO

(373) 1908 October 29 (No. 9020)

Advertisement (p. 4): 'Wanted, Birkenhead, from Jan. 1, Unfurnished Rooms for married couple, including cooking and all attendance; give terms and references. – By letter, Abercrombie, 47 Greenbank-rd., Birkenhead. 2372n4'

Also included in the issues of October 30 (9021), 31 (9022), November 2 (9023), 3 (9024), and 4 (9025).

LIVERPOOL POST AND MERCURY

He was probably approached by this paper to write reviews when he returned in 1919 to Liverpool to take up the post of Lecturer in Poetry to the University of Liverpool. All contributions are book reviews unless otherwise stated, all being signed in full, except one review which is initialled.

(374) 1919 October 1 (No. 20071)

(p. 7): *Heartbreak House*; *Great Catherine*; and *Playlets of the War*, by George Bernard Shaw.

(375) 1919 October 8 (No. 20077)

(p. 7): *The Problem of 'Hamlet'*, by the Right Hon. J. M. Robertson.

(376) 1919 October 22 (No. 20089)

(p. 7): *Some Diversions of a Man of Letters*, by Ermund [*sic*] Gosse.

(377) 1920 January 21 (No. 20165)

(p. 9): *Seven Men*, by Max Beerbohm.

(378) 1920 January 28 (No. 20171)

(p. 9): *Collected Poems of Thomas Hardy.*

(379) 1920 April 21 (No. 20242)

(p. 7): *A Brazilian Mystic*, by R. B. Cunningham Graham.

(380) 1920 May 12 (No. 20260)

(p. 7): *The Unfortunate Traveller*, by Thomas Nash; *Philip Massinger*, by A. H. Cruikshank.

(381) 1920 July 7 (No. 20308)

(p. 9): *Mother and Child*, drawings by Bernard Meninsky, text by Jan Gordon; *Epstein*, text by B. Van Dieren.

(382) 1920 November 3 (No. 20410)

(p. 7): *King Lear's Wife: and Other Plays*, by Gordon Bottomley.

(383) 1920 December 1 (No. 20434)

(p. 9): *A Survey of English Literature, 1830–1880*, by Oliver Elton.

(384) 1921 December 14 (No. 20755)

(p. 9): *Gruach and Britain's Daughter*, by Gordon Bottomley.

(385) 1922 December 29 (No. 21077)

Letter (p. 9): 'The Playhouse Pantomime', signed at 'The University, Liverpool, December 28, 1922'.

This was the first newspaper to which L. A. contributed. Charles, his brother, originally helped to get him the job; as he said in a letter of September 20, 1907: 'Charles writes this morning to say that he has got an appointment for me with the Editor of the City News on Monday next [September 23]. I don't expect it will lead to much, as it is a poor paper and I'm off journalism, since it is the custom to make you work at least a year for nothing, all for the honour and glory of writing "Journalist" on your visiting card. However it may lead to an occasional special, and no doubt I shall be well fed with wholesome advice.' He was offered book and play reviewing and the 'wholesome advice' at the interview, and was told he was to have unpaid work to begin with until the editor had seen what he was like as a reviewer. The editor was very pleased with his first review, of September 28, and from then on he was given play reviewing, which pleased L. A., especially as he considered he was being sent to the best plays in Manchester. On October 16, 1907, he was able at last to say 'the Editor is going to pay my expenses in the future'. Unfortunately there was no further mention of this paper in letters or elsewhere, and it is not known why he broke with it, but it might have been when he started contributing to the *Liverpool Courier* in January, 1908. As all contributions are unsigned, it is not possible to find any others than those mentioned in letters. This was a Saturday newspaper only.

(**386**) 1907 September 28 (No. 2284)

> Book review (p. 2): *The Court Theatre (1904–1907)*, by Desmond McCarthy.

(**387**) 1907 October 12 (No. 2286)

> Play review (p. 7): *Gentlemen of the Road*, by Charles McEvoy; *Widowers Houses*, by G. B. Shaw.
>
> Written October 9.

(**388**) 1907 October 19 (No. 2287)

> Play review (p. 7): *John Bull's Other Island*, by G. B. Shaw.
>
> Written October 15.

On January 8, 1910, he said, 'I mean to approach [the *Manchester Guardian*] as soon as possible. I saw an influencial man this morning who is going to write to Scott (editor M. G.) about me . . .'. He had intended to get on the staff, but the reply from Scott, received on February 12, said there were no vacancies at that time, but they would like to see more of his newspaper work, and he was asked to go to a personal interview. He had previously, on February 6, been offered reviewing from Monkhouse, literary editor, which at first he was inclined to decline. But at the interview where he saw both Scott and Monkhouse, he was obviously persuaded to change his mind. All contributions listed are book reviews, unless otherwise stated, all being signed by initials or in full. He started contributing unsigned material, probably all reviews, just after February 16, 1910, but none is traceable until his first signed review of March 9. There are probably many untraceable unsigned reviews between 1910 and 1914.

(389) 1910 March 9 (No. 19838)

    (p. 5): *Franklin Kane*, by Anne Douglas Sedgwick.

(390) 1910 March 30 (No. 19856)

    (p. 3): *The Island of Providence*, by Frederick Niven.

(391) 1910 April 13 (No. 19868)

    (p. 5): *Devious Ways*, by Gilbert Cannan.

(392) 1910 April 18 (No. 19872)

    (p. 5): *Sterne: A Study*, by Walter Sichel.

(393) 1910 April 20 (No. 19874)

    (p. 5): *The King's Highway*, by H. B. Marriott Watson.

(394) 1910 May 4 (No. 19886)

    (p. 5): *A Pilgramage of Truth*, by D. G. Peto.

(395) 1910 May 25 (No. 19904)

(p. 5): *The Will and the Way*, by Bernard Cape.

(396) 1910 June 15 (No. 19922)

(p. 5): *Cuthbert Learmont*, by J. A. Revermort.

(397) 1910 June 20 (No. 19926)

(p. 5): *A History of English Versification*, by Jakob Schipper.

(398) 1910 July 6 (No. 19940)

(p. 5): *The Other Side*, by Horace Annesley Vachell.

(399) 1910 July 11 (No. 19944)

(p. 5): *English Literature and Religion, 1800–1900*, by Edward Mortimer Chapman.

(400) 1910 August 1 (No. 19962)

(p. 3): *Mark Twain's Speeches*, introduced by William Dean Howells.

(401) 1910 August 5 (No. 19966)

(p. 5): *Walter Headlam, His Letters and Poems*, by Cecil Headlam.

(402) 1910 August 10 (No. 19970)

(p. 3): *Written in the Rain*, by John Trevena.

(403) 1910 August 23 (No. 19981)

(p. 5): *Literary Criticism from the Elizabethan Dramatists*, by David Klein.

(404) 1910 August 31 (No. 19988)

(p. 5): *Harmen Pols, Peasant*, by Maarten Maarten.

(405) 1910 November 2 (No. 20042)

(p. 5): *The Great Offender*, by Vincent Brown.

(405) 1910 November 9 (No. 20048)

(p. 7): *Martin the Mummer*, by Dorothy Margaret Stuart.

(407) 1910 November 16 (No. 20054)

(p. 5): *The Osbornes*, by E. F. Benson.

(408) 1910 November 23 (No. 20060)

(p. 5): *Fortuna Chance*, by James Prior.

(409) 1910 November 30 (No. 20066)

(p. 7): *The Island of Souls*, by M. Urquart.

(410) 1910 December 28 (No. 20090)

(p. 3): *Out of the Dark*, by the Countess of Cromartie.

(411) 1911 January 25 (No. 20114)

(p. 4): *The Usurper*, by William J. Locke.

(412) 1911 February 15 (No. 20132)

(p. 5): *A Deserted House*, by Elizabeth Stuart Phelps.

(413) 1911 March 8 (No. 20150)

(p. 5): *The Soundless Tide*, by F. E. Crichton.

(414) 1911 March 15 (No. 20156)

(p. 7): *The Lonely Road*, by A. E. Jacomb.

(415) 1911 March 23 (No. 20163)

(p. 5): *Mysticism*, by Evelyn Underhill.

(416) 1911 April 5 (No. 20174)

(p. 5): *The Dweller on the Threshold*, by Robert Hichen.

(417) 1911 April 7 (No. 20176)

(p. 5): *Ancient Lights and Certain New Reflections*, by Ford Madox Hueffer.

(418) 1911 April 12 (No. 20180)

(p. 5): *The Unknown God,* by Putnam Weale.

(419) 1911 April 19 (No. 20186)

(p. 5): *The Magic of the Hill: A Romance of Mont-martre,* by Duncan Schwann.

(420) 1911 May 10 (No. 20204)

(p. 5): *The Garden of Resurrection,* by E. Temple Thurston.

(421) 1911 May 31 (No. 20222)

(p. 7): *Oliver's Kind Woman,* by Philip Gibbs.

(422) 1911 June 12 (No. 20232)

(p. 5): *The Diary of Dr. John William Polidori, 1816,* edited by W. M. Rossetti.

(423) 1911 June 14 (No. 20234)

(p. 5): *The Broken Phial,* by Percy White.

(424) 1911 July 19 (No. 20264)

(p. 5): *The Shadow of Love,* by Marcelle Tinayre.

(425) 1911 July 26 (No. 20270)

(p. 5): *The Dawn of All,* by Robert Hugh Benson.

(426) 1911 August 16 (No. 20288)

(p. 5): *The Red Lantern,* by Edith Wherry.

(427) 1911 August 23 (No. 20294)

(p. 5): *Deborah,* by Agnes Grozier Herbertson.

(428) 1911 August 30 (No. 20300)

(p. 5): *Poppies in the Corn,* by Madame Albanesi.

(429) 1911 September 19 (No. 20317)

(p. 5): *Frederick James Furnivall: A Volume of Personal Record.*

(430) 1911 September 27 (No. 20324)

(p. 5): *The First Born*, by R. Murray Gilchrist.

(431) 1911 October 6 (No. 20332)

(p. 5): *English Poesy: An Introduction*, by W. Winslow Hall; *Poetry and Prose: Essays on Modern English Poetry*, by Adolphus Alfred Jack.

(432) 1911 October 12 (No. 20337)

(p. 4): *The Great Secret. A Book for Beginners;* and *Glimpses of the Next State*, by Vice Admiral W. Usborne Moore; *Psychical Research and Thought Transference*, by E. Eden Paul; *The Immediate Future, and Other Lectures*, by Annie Besant.

(433) 1911 December 27 (No. 20401)

(p. 3): *The Centaur*, by Algernon Blackwood.

(434) 1912 January 10 (No. 20413)

(p. 4): *Daughters of Ishmael*, by Reginald Wright Kauffman. Also *The Challenge*, by Harold Begbie. And *The Forward in Love*, by Richard Bird. And *The Motto of Mrs McLane*, by Shirley Carson.

(435) 1912 January 16 (No. 20418)

(p. 5): *Poets and Poetry*, by John Bailey.

(436) 1912 January 22 (No. 20423)

(p. 4): *The Rowley Poems of Thomas Chatterton*, with an introduction by Maurice Evan Hare.

(437) 1912 February 7 (No. 20437)

(p. 4): *The Principal Girl*, by J. C. Snaith. And *The*

Ship that Came Home in the Dark, by Agnes Grozier Herbertson.

(**438**) 1912 February 14 (No. 20443)

(p. 5): *The Man Who Could Not Lose,* by Richard Harding Davis.

(**439**) 1912 February 27 (No. 20454)

(p. 7): *The Early Literary Career of Robert Browning,* by Thomas R. Lounsbury.

(**440**) 1912 February 29 (No. 20456)

(p. 4): *The Poet and the Poetic Principle,* by L. Conrad Hartley.

(**441**) 1912 March 8 (No. 20463)

(p. 4): *Psychic Phenomena, Science and Immortality,* by Henry Frank; *The Evidence for the Supernatural,* by Ivor Tuckett.

(**442**) 1912 March 11 (No. 20465)

(p. 5): *The Future of Poetry,* by F. P. B. Osmaston.

(**443**) 1912 March 12 (No. 20466)

(p. 5): *The Problems of Philosophy,* by Bertrand Russell.

(**444**) 1912 March 13 (No. 20467)

(p. 5): *The Forest on the Hill,* by Eden Phillpotts.

(**445**) 1912 March 21 (No. 20474)

(p. 5): *The Story of Evolution,* by Joseph McCabe.

(**446**) 1912 March 26 (No. 20478)

(p. 4): *The People's Books.*
Letter (p. 7): 'Futurism', dated March 23.

(447) 1912 March 27 (No. 20479)

(p. 7): *Little Brother*, by Gilbert Cannan.

(448) 1912 May 2 (No. 20510)

(p. 5): *Défense de la Poésie Français, à l'Usage des Lecteures Anglaise*, par Emile Legouis.

(449) 1912 May 8 (No. 20515)

(p. 7): *The Night Land*, by William Hope Hodgson.

(450) 1912 May 15 (No. 20521)

(p. 7): *Love's Pilgramage*, by Upton Sinclair.

(451) 1912 May 16 (No. 20522)

(p. 4): *The Clouds*, by Charles M. Doughty.

(452) 1912 June 5 (No. 20539)

(p. 5): *The Ghost Ship and Other Stories*, by Richard Middleton.

(453) 1912 June 12 (No. 20545)

(p. 5): *Blinds Down: A Chronicle of Charminster*, by [Horace Annesley] Vachell.

(454) 1912 July 1 (No. 20561)

(p. 7): *The Widow in the Bye Street*, by John Masefield.

(455) 1912 July 3 (No. 20563)

(p. 7): *Amor Vincit*, by Mrs. R. S. Garnett.

(456) 1912 July 4 (No. 20564)

(p. 7): *The Temptation of St. Anthony*, by Gustav Flaubert.

(457) 1912 August 26 (No. 20609)

(p. 5): *English Lyrical Poetry: From Its Origins to the Present Time*, by Edward Bliss.

(458) 1912 September 25 (No. 20635)

(p. 5): *The Turnstile*, by A. E. W. Mason.

(459) 1912 October 8 (No. 20646)

(p. 4): *Essays and Studies in English Literature*, by S. J. Mary Suddard.

(460) 1912 October 30 (No. 20665)

(p. 6): *John of Jingalo*, by Laurence Housman. Also *The Olympian*, by James Oppenheim.

(461) 1912 November 6 (No. 20671)

(p. 7): *The Crock of Gold*, by James Stephens.

(462) 1912 November 19 (No. 20682)

(p. 7): *Poetical Works of Robert Bridges.*

(463) 1912 November 20 (No. 20683)

(p. 7): *The Nest*, by Anne Douglas Sedgwick. Also *Fate Knocks at the Door*, by Will Levington Comfort.

(464) 1912 November 21 (No. 20684)

(p. 7): *The People's Books.*

(465) 1912 November 26 (No. 20688)

(p. 6): *The Complete Works of George Savile, the First Marquis of Halifax*, edited by Walter Raleigh.

(466) 1912 November 27 (No. 20689)

(p. 7): *Broken Pitchers*, by Reginald Wright Kauffman.

(467) 1912 December 10 (No. 20700)

(p. 6): *Main Currents of Modern Thought*, by Rudolf Euken.

(468) 1912 December 17 (No. 20706)

(p. 6): *Collected Verses of Rudyard Kipling.*

(469) 1913 January 6 (No. 20722)

(p. 5): *The Oxford Book of Victorian Verse*, edited by Sir Arthur Quiller-Couch; *Georgian Poetry, 1911–1912*, edited by Edward Marsh.

(470) 1913 January 14 (No. 20729)

(p. 7): *Gitanjali*, by Rabindra Nath Tagore.

(471) 1913 January 24 (No. 20738)

(p. 7): *The Making of Poetry: A Critical Study of Its Nature and Value*, by Dr. Arthur H. R. Fairchild.

(472) 1913 February 4 (No. 20747)

(p. 7): *The Life of a Spider*, by J. Henri Fabre.

(473) 1913 February 11 (No. 20753)

(p. 7): *Algernon Charles Swinburne: A Critical Study*, by Edward Thomas.

(474) 1913 February 17 (No. 20758)

(p. 7): *Primitiae: Essays in English Literature*, by students of the University of Liverpool.

(475) 1913 February 18 (No. 20759)

(p. 7): *Later Poems*, by Alexander Anderson.

(476) 1913 February 20 (No. 20761)

(p. 4): *Vital Lies*, by Vernon Lee.

(477) 1913 March 3 (No. 20770)

(p. 7): *The Home University Library.*

(478) 1913 March 7 (No. 20774)

(p. 5): *The Day Before Yesterday*, by Richard Middleton; *Poems and Songs*, by Richard Middleton.

(479) 1913 March 18 (No. 20783)

(p. 7): *The Influence of Baudelaire in France and England*, by G. Turquet-Milnes.

(480) 1913 March 19 (No. 20784)

(p. 4): *The Adventures of Dr. Whitty*, by George A. Birmingham.

(481) 1913 March 21 (No. 20786)

(p. 5): *The People's Books.*

(482) 1913 March 26 (No. 20790)

(p. 5): *The Weaker Vessel*, by E. F. Benson.

(483) 1913 April 16 (No. 20808)

(p. 5): *An Inn Upon the Road*, by Janet Dodge.

(484) 1913 April 21 (No. 20812)

(p. 5): *Thirty Indian Songs from the Punjab and Kashmir* edited by Ratan Devi.

(485) 1913 April 30 (No. 20820)

(p. 5): *Succession*, by Ethel Sidgwick.

(486) 1913 May 1 (No. 20821)

(p. 7): *Love Poems and Others*, by D. H. Lawrence.

(487) 1913 May 12 (No. 20830)

(p. 5): *Dauber*, by John Masefield.

(488) 1913 May 14 (No. 20832)

(p. 5): *Michael Ferrys*, by Mrs. Henry de la Pasture.

(489) 1913 May 22 (No. 20839)

(p. 6): *Swinburne: An Estimate*, by John Drinkwater.

(490) 1913 May 27 (No. 20843)

(p. 6): *The Invincible Alliance and Other Essays*, by Francis Grierson.

(491) 1913 June 2 (No. 20848)

(p. 7): *The English Lyric*, by Felix Schelling.

(492) 1913 June 6 (No. 20852)

(p. 7): *The People's Books*.

(493) 1913 June 9 (No. 20854)

(p. 5): *The Fellowship Books*.

(494) 1913 June 10 (No. 20855)

(p. 6): *The Icknield Way*, by Edward Thomas.

(495) 1913 June 11 (No. 20856)

(p. 7): *Unpath'd Waters*, by Frank Harris.

(496) 1913 June 30 (No. 20872)

(p. 7): *Poems*, by Alice Meynell.

(497) 1913 July 2 (No. 20874)

(p. 7): *Sons and Lovers*, by D. H. Lawrence.

(498) 1913 July 23 (No. 20892)

(p. 5): *One Woman's Life*, by Robert Herrick.

(499) 1913 July 24 (No. 20893)

(p. 5): *Tales of the Mermaid Tavern*, by Alfred Noyes.

(500) 1913 August 4 (No. 20902)

(p. 4): *The Works of Francis Thompson*.

(501) 1913 August 6 (No. 20904)

(p. 4): *The Sentence of Silence*, by Reginald Wright Kauffman.

(502) 1913 August 14 (No. 20911

    (p. 5): *Collected Literary Essays, Classical and Modern*, by A. W. Verrall; *Collected Studies in Greek and Latin Scholarship*, by A. W. Verrall.

(503) 1913 August 21 (No. 20917)

    (p. 5): *Plays*, by Arthur Strindberg, translated by Edwin Bjorkman; *Plays*, by Arthur Strindberg, translated by Edith and Warner Oland; *Easter*, by A. Strindberg; *Advent*, by A. Strindberg.

(504) 1913 August 29 (No. 20924)

    (p. 5): *A Mainsail Haul*; and *Saltwater Ballads*, by John Masefield.

(505) 1913 September 3 (No. 20928)

    (p. 5): *Sinister Street*, by Compton Mackenzie.

(506) 1913 September 17 (No. 20940)

    (p. 5): *Valentine*, by Grant Richards.

(507) 1913 October 14 (No. 20963)

    (p. 6): *Everyman's Library*.

(508) 1913 October 15 (No. 20964)

    (p. 4): *Ellen Adair*, by Frederick Niven.

(509) 1913 October 16 (No. 20965)

    (p. 6): *The Daffodil Fields*, by John Masefield.

(510) 1913 October 27 (No. 20974)

    (p. 7): *Songs from Books*, by Rudyard Kipling.

(511) 1913 October 28 (No. 20975)

    (p. 6): *Rudolph Eucken: His Philosophy and Influence*, by Meyrick Booth.

(512) 1913 October 31 (No. 20978)

(p. 7): *Collected Poems*, by A. E. [George William Russell].

(513) 1913 November 3 (No. 20980)

(p. 6): *Lucky Pehr*, by August Strindberg.

(514) 1913 November 13 (No. 20989)

(p. 4): *Diderot as a Disciple of English Thought*, by R. Loyalty Cru.

(515) 1913 November 18 (No. 20993)

(p. 6): *Lyric Poetry*, by Ernest Rhys.

(516) 1913 November 25 (No. 20999)

(p. 5): *The People's Books*.

(517) 1913 December 3 (No. 21006)

(p. 7): *The Book of Martha*, by Mrs. Dowdall.

(518) 1914 February 18 (No. 21071)

(p. 7): *The Making of an Englishman*, by W. L. George.

(519) 1914 February 24 (No. 21076)

(p. 6): *Essays and Studies by Members of the English Association*, collected by C. H. Herford.

(520) 1914 March 11 (No. 21089)

(p. 6): *Life is a Dream*, by Richard Curle.

(521) 1914 March 13 (No. 21091)

(p. 6): *Through the Toril*, by Yone Noguchi.

(522) 1914 March 24 (No. 21100)

(p. 6): *Lectures on Dryden*, by A. W. Verrall.

(523) 1914 April 2 (No. 21108)

(p. 6): *Human Quintessence*, by Sigurd Ibsen.

(524) 1914 April 16 (No. 21120)

(p. 4): *The Origin of Attic Comedy*, by F. M. Cornford.

(525) 1914 April 24 (No. 21127)

(p. 6): *Shakespeare Personally*, by David Masson.

(526) 1914 May 7 (No. 21138)

(p. 6): *The Sea is Kind*, by T. Sturge Moore.

(527) 1914 May 11 (No. 21141)

(p. 6): *Plays*, by August Strindberg.

(528) 1914 May 14 (No. 21144)

(p. 6): *The People's Books*.

(529) 1914 May 26 (No. 21154)

(p. 6): *The Fire of Love*; and *The Mending of Life*, by Richard Rolle.

(530) 1914 May 27 (No. 21155)

(p. 6): *The Death of a Nobody*, by Jules Romains.

(531) 1914 June 12 (No. 21169)

(p. 6): *Science and Method*, by Henri Poincaré.

(532) 1914 June 24 (No. 21179)

(p. 7): *Love's Legend*, by H. Fielding-Hall.

(533) 1914 July 6 (No. 21189)

(p. 6): *The Spirit of Japanese Poetry*, by Yone Noguchi.

(534) 1914 July 8 (No. 21191)

(p. 6): *The Royal Runway*; and *Jingalo in Revolution: A Sequel to 'John of Jingalo'*, by Laurence Housman.

(535) 1914 July 9 (No. 21192)

(p. 7): *Joseph Conrad: A Study*, by Richard Curle.

(536) 1914 July 13 (No. 21195)

(p. 7): *The Architecture of Humanism*, by Geoffrey Scott.

(537) 1914 July 17 (No. 21199)

(p. 7): *Blast: Review of the Great English Vortex*, edited by Wyndham Lewis.

(538) 1914 July 22 (No. 21203)

(p. 6): *Bridget Considine*, by Mary Crosbie.

(539) 1914 July 31 (No. 21211)

(p. 6): *Know Your Own Mind*, by William Glover.

At 11 o'clock on August 4, 1914 Britain declared war on Germany. From August 5, the column 'new books' was discontinued, and the space devoted to war news.

(540) 1925 December 2 (Supplement to no. 24736)

Article (p. v): *Perfect Moments*.

Reprinted in *Littell's Living Age*, q.v. (**261**).

THE MICROCOSM

(541) 1924 Summer (Vol. IX, No. 1)

Poem (p. 2): *White Love (Out of Sidi Hammo)*.

For notes on this, see *Twelve Idyls* (**28**).

THE MODERN LANGUAGE REVIEW

(542) 1933 April (Vol. XXVIII, No. 2)

Book review (pp. 262–264): *The Letters of Robert Burns*, edited by J. de Lancey Ferguson.

(543) 1935 April (Vol. XXX, No. 2)

Book review (pp. 237–238): *English Poetry in the Late Nineteenth Century*, by B. Ifor Evans.

MORNING POST

(544) 1915 April 27 (No. 44598)

Obituary (p. 6): *The Late Rupert Brooke: England's Poet Soldier.*

Reprinted in *The Handsomest Young Man in England*, by Michael Hastings (London: Michael Joseph, 1967; p. 185).

(545) 1921 December 9 (No. 46658)

Article (p. 4): *Modern Poetry.*

The poem 'The Nightingale' appeared for the first time in this article; later published in *Twelve Idyls*, q.v. **(28)**.

(546) 1921 December 30 (No. 46675)

Article (p. 8): *Modern Poetry. Tennyson and Browning.*

THE NATION

On November 18, 1907, L. A. wrote from Cambridge saying G. Lowes Dickinson had written to the editor of the *Nation* with a view to getting him some kind of work, and on November 20, L. A. received a letter from them requesting a specimen of his poetry. He got to work immediately on 'Soul and Body', sending it to them the next day. The poem was accepted, and at the same time they asked for an article, particularly on 'some scientific subject treated from the imaginative point of view' (this had been L.A.'s suggestion to them in his letter sent with the poem). The outcome was the article 'The World as a Tune', and probably others that were never published.

After the first contributions of poetry, they seemed to lose interest in his work, except for reviews and the very occasional article which he continued to do for them until about the beginning of the First World War. Very few of his contributions are to be found, all being unsigned (except the three poems and article 'The World as a Tune', which are signed in full, and one review signed by initials). All others have been traced from letters.

(547) 1907 November 30 (Vol. II, No. 9)

Poem (p. 309): *Soul and Body.*

For notes, see *Interludes and Poems* (1).

(548) 1908 January 4 (Vol. II, No. 14)

Poem (p. 498): *The Trance.*

For notes, see *Interludes and Poems* (1).

(549) 1908 February 8 (Vol. II, No. 19)

Poem (p. 679): *Hope and Despair.*

For notes, see *Interludes and Poems* (1).

(550) 1908 March 21 (Vol. II, No. 25)

Article (p. 897–898): *The World as a Tune.*

(551) 1908 July 11 (Vol. III, No. 15)

Book review (pp. 540–546): [probably not all by L. A.] *The Fourth Ship*, by Miss Mayne; *A Man of Genius*, by Miss Willcocks; *My Son and I*, by Mrs. M. H. Spielman; *The Flemings*, by unknown author; *The Bishop's Scapegoat*, by Mr. Clegg; *The White Wedding*, by M. P. Shiel; *The Dual Heritage*, by Mabel Godfrey-Faussett; *The Key of the Door*, by R. Ramsey; *The Human Boy Again*, by Eden Phillpotts; *The Thief on the Cross*, by Mrs. Harold Gorst; *Anne Page*, by Netta Syrett; *Angela's Marriage*, by Miss Moberly; *Keepers of the House*, by Richard Pryce; *A Suburban Scandal*, by Gurner Gillman; *The Last Shore*, by Vincent Brown; *Love's Shadow*, by Ada Leverson; *The Woman Who Vowed*, by Ellison

Harding; *Dominy's Dollars*, by B. Paul Neuman; *Armadin: A Tale of Old Winchester*, by Alfred Boroker.

(552) 1908 August 1 (Vol. III, No. 18)

Book review (pp. 645–646): *New Poems*, by St. John Lucas; *Mont St. Michel and Other Poems*, by Roland Thirlmere; *A Ballad of a Great City and Other Poems*, by David Lowe; *The Sorrowful Princess*, by Eva Gore-Booth; *Ballads and Lyrics of Socialism*, by E. Nesbit; *The Morning of Life*, by Augustus Ralli; *The Knocking at the Door and Other Poems*, by Alice Maddock; *A Modern Judas and Other Rhymes*, by E. Vincent; *Songs of the Uplands*, by Alice Law; *The Vigil of Brunhild*, by Frederic Manning; *West Country Verses*, by Arthur L. Salmon; *Talmudic Legends; Hymns and Paraphrases*, by Alice Lucas; *A Painter's Pastime*, by Margaret Thomas.

Received for review on June 24; nine were written on about June 29, the remaining four on July 2.

(553) 1908 November 14 (Vol. IV, No. 7)

Book review (pp. 280–282): *Arvat: A Dramatic Poem*, by Leopold H. Myers; *The Tragedy of Saint Elizabeth of Hungary*, by Arthur Dillon; *The Mask of the Grail*, by Ernest Rhys; *The Song of the Manly Men*, by Frank Hudson; *The Autumn Garden*, by Edmund Gosse; *The Mockers*, by Jane Barlow; *Nature Poems*, by William H. Davies; *London Visions*, by Laurence Binyon.

Written probably November 7.

(554) 1908 December 19 (Vol. IV, No. 12)

Book review (p. 475): probably *The Oxford Thackeray*, introduced by George Saintsbury.

(555) 1909 January 30 (Vol. IV, No. 18)

Book review (pp. 681–682): *The Testament of John Davidson*, by Grant Richards; *The Dowager of Jerusalem*, by Reginald Farrer; *Queen Mariamne*, by the author of 'Borgia' [Michael Field]; *Songs of Good Fighting*, by Eugene R. White; *Dramatic Odes and Rhapsodies*, by F. P. B. Osmaston; *A Shropshire Lad*, by A. E. Housman; *Thysia: An Elegy*, by anon.; *The Call of Dawn*, by Esmé C. Wingfield-Stratford.

Books received by L. A. on November 21; the reviews being written about December 10, 1908.

(556) 1909 June 19 (Vol. V, No. 12)

Book review (pp. 430–431): *The Immortal Hour*, by Fiona Macleod; *Undine*, by Whitworth Wynne; *Lyrical and other Poems*, by John Drinkwater; *Day Dreams of Greece*, by Charles Wharton Stork; *The Story of Amaryllis*, by Viola Taylor; *Shelley: a Dramatic Poem*, by Claude Edward Foster; *Towards the Uplands*, by Lloyd Mifflin; *Experiences*, by Katherine Tynan.

(557) 1910 February 19 (Vol. VI, No. 21)

Article (pp. 803–804): probably *Bread and Games*.

Written February 9.

(558) 1912 January 27 (Vol. X, No. 17)

Book review (pp. 717–718): *A Sicilian Idyll*; and *Judith*, by T. Sturge Moore.

(559) 1914 June 13 (Vol. XV, No. 11)

Book review (pp. 423–424): *North of Boston*, by Robert Frost.

Excerpts from this review appeared in 'The Listener' column of the *Boston Evening Transcript*, q.v. (**209**).

(**560**) 1923 December 29 (Vol. XXXIV, No. 13)

Book review (p. 491): *The Famous Tragedy of the Queen of Cornwall,* by Thomas Hardy.

NEW NUMBERS

(**561**) 1914 New Numbers | Wilfrid Wilson Gibson | Rupert Brooke | Lascelles Abercrombie | John Drinkwater | PUBLISHED AT | RYTON, DYMOCK, GLOU-CESTER.

Format: Crown 4to, $9\frac{3}{4} \times 7\frac{1}{4}$ ins.

Collation: 60 pages [Vol. 1, No. 1], consisting of:—
half-title, verso blank (pp. 1–2); title page, verso blank (pp. 3–4); pages 5–59, text; page 60 blank.

Binding: dove-grey paper wrapper; black lettering on front cover; imprint on outside back cover; no end papers; all edges cut. (A note [*Books by the same writers*] was added to the inside back cover of the second impression of No. 1, and Nos. 2–4).

Signatures: A^8 B–C^8 D^6.

Note: the other three issues are on identical lines as above, except the signatures: No. 2, pages 61–108 (*iv* + 48 pages), A^8 B–C^8 D^2; No. 3, pages 109–152 (*iv* + 44 pages), A^8 B–C^8; No. 4, pages 153–212 (*iv* + 60 pages) [with index], unsigned [actually A–D^8].
The contributor's names are on the title page in the order they appear in the text. They changed order each issue.

Publication: February, 1914 (Vol. 1, No. 1) [actually published March (8?), 1914]. A second impression was printed later that year, noted 'Second Edition' on the cover.

Contribution: Dramatic poem (pp. 31–54): *The Olympians.* For notes on this, see *Twelve Idyls* (**28**).

(562) 1914   *Publication*: April, 1914 (Vol. 1, No. 2) [actually published probably in May, 1914].

> *Contribution:* Poetic drama (pp. 61–96): *The End of the World.*
> For notes, see *Four Short Plays* (**18**).

(563) 1914   New Numbers | *A Quarterly Publication of the Poems of* | Rupert Brooke | John Drinkwater | Wilfrid Wilson Gibson | Lascelles Abercrombie | PUBLISHED AT | RYTON, DYMOCK, GLOUCESTER.

> *Publication:* August, 1914 (Vol. 1, No. 3) [actually probably published October, 1914].

> *Contribution:* Poem (pp. 147–152): *The Innocents.*
> For notes, see *Twelve Idyls* (**28**).

(564) 1915   *Publication:* December, 1914 (Vol. 1, No. 4) [actually published
[1914]   February (28?), 1915].

> *Contribution:* Poetic drama (pp. 170–191): *The Staircase.*
> For notes, see *Four Short Plays* (**18**).

This periodical, which lasted four issues only, has been detailed in full because of its importance.

In 1913 the idea for a quarterly of new poetry was suggested, with 'The New Shilling Garland' to be its title (the title being chosen by L. A. and W. Gibson; the Shilling Garland had been a series of ten booklets of verse, edited by Laurence Binyon). This name was disliked, and it was to have been changed to 'The Gallows Garland', possibly suggested by R. Brooke, after the name of the house where L. A. lived and where it was to be published. The name was now not liked by the others (including Edward Marsh, who was to become the collector of subscriptions), and so the name became 'New Numbers' by mutual agreement.

By the end of July, 1913, the pre-publication forms, probably written by L. A. or his wife, Catherine, were ready for distribution. They read: 'Should enough subscriptions be received to cover the cost of production, it is proposed to issue a Quarterly

Garland, entitled, 'NEW NUMBERS', devoted exclusively to the publication of new poems by Lascelles Abercrombie, Rupert Brooke, John Drinkwater, and Wilfrid Wilson Gibson. The subscription for the four issues will be 7/6; the price of separate issues will be 2/6. It is hoped to begin publication in January, 1914.' A subscription form was attached. It was sent from Wilfrid Gibson's house, The Old Nail-Shop, The Greenway, Ledbury, Herefordshire.

By December 13, 1913 they had over 200 subscriptions; by the last issue, they had over 500. On October 23, 1914, L. A. said in a letter: 'New Numbers has decided to come to an end. Rupert is fighting – he is just back from Antwerp. Wilfred finds he can make more money elsewhere. And I don't seem to hoist any poetry out these days.'

THE NEW STATESMAN AND NATION

(565)   1936   August 22 (Vol. XII [new series], No. 287)

> Letter (pp. 250–251): 'Britain and the Spanish War', signed by L. A., Norman Angell, Ernest Barker, P. M. S. Blackett, A. M. Carr Saunders, G. D. H. Cole, F. M. Cornford, C. Day Lewis, C. Delisle Burns, E. M. Forster, Margery Fry, G. T. Garrett, G. P. Gooch, Charlotte Haldane, J. B. S. Haldane, Hastings, R. H. Hodgkin, W. Horsfall Carter, Julian S. Huxley, Hewlett Johnson, David Low, F. L. Lucas, Geoffrey Mander, G. E. Moore, Gilbert Murray, Henry W. Nevinson, Rhonnda, Shena D. Simon, R. H. Tawney, H. G. Wells, Ralph Vaughan Williams, Leonard Woolf, Virginia Woolf – '23 Haymarket, W.'

THE NEW WEEKLY

(566)   1914   March 28 (Vol. I, No. 2)

> Book review (p. 58): *Neitzsche, and Other Exponents of Individualism*, by Paul Carus.

(567) 1914 April 4 (Vol. I, No. 3)

Book review (p. 88): *Lectures on Dryden,* delivered by A. W. Verrall.

(568) 1914 April 18 (Vol. I, No. 5)
Article (p. 138): *The Age and Poetry.*

(569) 1914 May 23 (Vol. I, No. 10)

Book review (pp. 313–314): *The Problem of Human Life,* by Rudolph Eucken; *The Spiritual Philosophy,* by Rev. J. Gurnhill.

(570) 1914 June 6 (Vol. I, No. 12)

Book review (p. 378): *Collected Essays of Rudolph Eucken,* edited by Meyrick Booth.

(571) 1914 July 4 (Vol. II, No. 16)

Book review (p. 89): *A Cluster of Grapes: a Book of Twentieth Century Poetry,* collated by Galloway Kyle; *The Rose of Ravenna,* by Edward A. Vidler; *Ballads of Old Bristol,* by Rose E. Sharland; *Ballads and Burdens,* by V. Goldie; *The Brood of Light,* by C. R. Crowther.

(572) 1914 August 1 (Vol. II, No. 20)

Book review (p. 212): *In Defence of What Might Be,* by Edward Holmes.

NINETEENTH CENTURY AND AFTER

(573) 1930 May (Vol. CVII, No. 639)

Article (pp. 716–728): *T. E. Brown.*

THE OBSERVER

(574) 1926 November 21 (No. 7069)

Book review (p. 7): *Collected Poems, 1905–1925,* by Wilfrid Gibson.

THE PARENTS' REVIEW

(575) 1922 August (Vol. XXXIII, No. 8)

Article (pp. 585–596): *Literature – Tyranny or Freedom.*

Taken from a lecture as read to the Parents' National Education Union, Big School, Westminster, London, at their annual meeting, May 26, 1922.

POETRY AND DRAMA

(576) 1913 March (Vol. 1, No. 1)

Poetic drama (pp. 100–119): *The Adder.*

For notes, see *Four Short Plays* (**18**).

(577) 1913 September (Vol. 1, No. 3)

Article (pp. 313–318): *Robert Bridges.*

(578) 1914 June (Vol. II, (No. II), No. 6)

Poetic drama extract (pp. 190–191): *The End of the World.*

Included in the main feature 'Extracts from recent poetry', the lines extracted are Act II, lines 71–120. For notes, see *Four Short Plays* (**18**).

(579) 1914 December (Vol. II, (No. IV), No. 8)

Book review (pp. 390–391): *Singsongs of the War,* by Maurice Hewlett; *A Ballad of 'The Gloster' and 'The Goeben',* by Maurice Hewlett; *Children of Love,* by Harold Monro.

THE POETRY REVIEW

(580) 1912 March (Vol. I, No. III)

Article (pp. 107–118): *The Function of Poetry in the Drama.*

'A paper read before the English Association in Manchester.'

The lecture was given at the end of December, 1911. Later published in *English Critical Essays*, q.v. (**128**).

(**581**) 1912 April (Vol. I, No. IV)

Article (pp. 168–170): *John Drinkwater: An Appreciation.*

(**582**) 1912 May (Vol. I, No. V)

Book review (p. 227): *The Way of the Lord*, by Elizabeth Gibson Cheyne.

(**583**) 1912 June (Vol. I, No. VI)

Book review (pp. 275–276): *Storm Song and Other Poems*, by Pallister Barkas.

(**584**) 1912 November (Vol. I, No. XI)

Book review (pp. 510–511): *The Vigil of Venus and Other Poems*, by 'Q' [Sir Arthur Quiller-Couch].

(**585**) 1912 December (Vo. I, No. XII)

Dramatic poem (pp. 529–533): *The Six Men of Calais.*

For notes, see *Twelve Idyls* (**28**).

THE PROCEEDINGS OF THE BRITISH ACADEMY

(**586**) 1930 [Annual] (Vol. XVI)

Article (pp. 137–164): *A Plea for the Liberty of Interpreting.*

The Annual Shakespeare Lecture delivered to the British Academy in London, May 7, 1930. It was issued separately from the *Proceedings* in a 32 page pamphlet. Later printed in *Selected Modern English Essays*, q.v. (**124**), and *Aspects of Shakespeare*, q.v. (**126**).

PROCEEDINGS OF THE LEEDS PHILOSOPHICAL AND LITERARY SOCIETY: LITERARY AND HISTORICAL SECTION

(**587**) 1928 November (Vol. II, Part I)

Article (pp. 1–5): *Drowsie Frighted Steeds.*

Issued separately from the *Proceedings* in an 8 page pamphlet.

PROCEEDINGS OF THE ROYAL INSTITUTION
(**588**) 1937 [February] (Vol. XXIX, No. 138)

Article (pp. 444–462): *Thomas Hardy's 'The Dynasts'.*

A lecture as read to the Royal Institution of Great Britain on January 15, 1937. It was issued separately in a twenty page pamphlet.

THE QUARTERLY REVIEW
(**589**) 1915 October (Vol. 224, No. 445, Article VI)

Article (pp. 395–414): *The War and the Poets.*

This is an expansion of book reviews. Reprinted in *Littell's Living Age*, q.v. (**260**).

THE REANDEAN NEWS SHEET
(**590**) [1923] (Vol. 1, No. 1)

Article (pp. 14–15): *The Drama of John Masefield.*

THE REVIEW OF ENGLISH STUDIES
(**591**) 1935 April (Vol. XV, No. 42)

Book review (pp. 220–221): *The Oxford Book of Sixteenth Century Verse*, edited by E. K. Chambers.

RHYTHM
(**592**) 1913 January (Vol. II, No. XII)

Tale (pp. 350–352): *The Wedding Ring.*

SCIENCE PROGRESS
(**593**) 1933 January (Vol. 27, No. 107)

Article (pp. 393–395): *Ronald Ross as a Poet.*

(594) 1922 July (Vol. VI, No. 3)

Poetic drama (pp. 237–254): *The Deserter*.

For notes, see *Four Short Plays* **(18)**.

THE TIMES

(595) 1916 July 28 (No. 41231)

Letter (p. 9): 'A Kitchener Memorial'.

(596) 1933 October 18 (No. 46578)

Letter (p. 10): 'Woman Teachers in Universities. Posts After Marriage', signed by L. A., Vera Brittain, J. B. S. Haldane, Winifred Holtby, Hilda Johnstone, Harold J. Laski, John MacMurray, Elizabeth Robins, Sybil Thorndike, R. H. Tawney.

(597) 1934 April 5 (No. 46720)

Letter (p. 6): 'The Money System. Industry and Orthodox Finance', signed by L. A., Bonamy Dobree, T. S. Eliot, Aldous Huxley, Hewlett Johnson, Edwin Muir, Hamish Miles, Herbert Read, I. A. Richards.

(598) 1934 May 10 (No. 46750)

Letter (extracts) (p. 10): 'The Monetary System', signed by the same as April 5 **(597)**.

(599) 1936 February 7 (No. 47292)

Letter (p. 15): 'Persecution of the Jews. Cultural Relations with Germany', signed by L. A., P. M. S. Blackett, G. D. H. Cole, Margery Fry, W. E. Le Gros Clark, Margaret Gardiner (Hon. Secretary) – 'Academic Freedom Committee, 110, Heath Street, N. W. 3., Feb. 5.'

(600) 1936 February 11 (No. 47295)

Obituary (p. 16): on Miss Ethel Boyce.

(601) 1936 August 19 (No. 47457)

Letter (p. 6): 'The Vortex in Spain. Issues of the Conflict', signed by L. A., Norman Angell, Ernest Barker, P. M. S. Blackett, A. M. Carr Saunders, F. M. Cornford, C. Day Lewis, C. Delisle Burns, E. M. Forster, Margery Fry, G. T. Garrett, G. P. Gooch, Charlotte Haldane, J. B. S. Haldane, Hastings, W. Horsfall Carter, Julian S. Huxley, Hewlett Johnson, David Low, F. L. Lucas, G. E. Moore, Gilbert Murray, Henry W. Nevinson, Rhonnda, Shena D. Simon, R. H. Tawney, H. G. Wells, Ralph Vaughan Williams, Leonard Woolf, Virginia Woolf.

Dated August 18.

(602) 1936 September 28 (No. 47491)

Letter (p. 8): 'Afforestation in the Lake District', signed by L. A., Aberdare, Balniel, W. H. Beveridge, J. W. Burns-Lindow, Helen Darbishire, John Dower, Reginald Lennard, J. A. Lichfield, W. Nunn, Claude Petriburg, Eileen Power, Wilfred Roberts, H. Graham White.

(603) 1936 December 24 (No. 47566)

Letter (p. 8): 'Forestry in the Lake District. Preservation of the Valleys', signed by L. A., Aberdare, Balniel, William Beveridge, J. Burns-Lindow, Howard of Penrith, Reginald Lennard, J. A. Lichfield, W. Nunn, Claude Petriburg, Eillen Power, H. Graham White – 'Friends of the Lake District'.

(604) 1962 May 28 (No. 55402)

Obituary (p. 14): *Mr. Wilfrid Gibson. Trenchant Poet of the Poor.*

L. A. almost certainly contributed a large portion of this obituary.

THE TIMES EDUCATIONAL SUPPLEMENT

(605) 1915 February 2 (No. 54)

Letter (p. 26): 'German Frankness'.

THE TIMES LITERARY SUPPLEMENT

Although very little can be found in this paper, all contributions being unsigned, he did contribute many reviews and some leading articles.

(606) 1915 June 10 (No. 699)

Poem (p. 190): *The Lover in Wartime.*

For notes, see 'April 13th, 1915' in *Lyrics and Unfinished Poems* **(40)**.

(607) 1917 August 17 (No. 813)

Leading article (pp. 385–386): *Views and Fairies.*

This was later revised and expanded for the first lecture of *Romanticism*, q.v. **(26)**.

(608) 1934 May 3 (No. 1683)

Letter (p. 322): 'Dickens and Jorrocks'.

(609) 1936 April 11 (No. 1784)

Letter (p. 316): 'Milton Sonnet XVII'.

THE TOWN PLANNING REVIEW

(610) 1915 October (Vol. V , No. 2)

Book review (pr. 137–142): *Cities in Evolution: An Introduction to the Town Planning Movement and to the Study of Civics,* by Patrick Geddes.

(611) 1921 July (Vol. IX, No. 2)

Book review (pp. 125–127): *The Things Which are Seen: A Revaluation of the Visual Arts,* by A. Trystan Edwards.

This periodical lasted three issues only. The contributors were all anonymous, but due to the insight of someone connected with it, the initials of the contributors were marked against many of the items in the copies examined. It is possible that some un-initialled contributions are by L. A.; a few have been recognised as probably by him, but are not confirmable, marked below with ★. Contributions by L. A. were never published again, unless otherwise stated, all of them probably being written near the date of publication here.

(**612**) 1902 'Midsummer' (No. 1)

> Poem (pp. 5–8): *An Imperfect Painter.*
>
> 132 lines.
>
> Poem (p. 8): *Farewell.*
>
> Two stanza poem of 12 lines.
>
> Poem (p. 11): *To Idleness.*
>
> Seven stanza poem of 28 lines.
>
> Poetic drama (pp. 21–27): *Scene from a Verse Comedy.*
>
> Pre-scene, 15 lines; 'Act II, Scene III', 229 lines.
>
> ★Poem (p. 28): *To Evening Primroses.*
>
> Two stanza poem of 14 lines.
>
> Prose dialogue (pp. 31–35): *Famine and Pestilence. A Dialogue.*
>
> Later printed in *Speculative Dialogues*, q.v. (**12**).
>
> Poem (p. 38): *The Fear.*
>
> Later printed in *Interludes and Poems*, q.v. (**1**).
>
> ★Prose dialogue (pp. 47–48): *Samuel Johnson, Ll.D., On Painting.*
>
> This is almost certainly by L. A.

(613) 1902 November (No. 2)

Tale (pp. 4–8): *Devil's Man.*

Later printed in the *Bulletin of the Sandon Studios Society*, q.v. (**216**).

Poem (p. 9): [*Ode*] *To Faunus.*

Three stanza poem of 34 lines.

★Tale (pp. 15–21): *The Princess of Thrabe.*

(614) 1903 May (No. 3)

Tale (pp. 4–10): *The Case of the Late Poet Laureate.*

Subdivided into five parts, numbered 1 to 5.

★Poem (p. 10): *Rondeau.*

A poem of three stanzas, 15 lines.

THE VINEYARD

(615) 1911 May (No. 8)

Poem (pp. 556–557): *The Stream's Song.*

For notes on this, see *Twelve Idyls* (**28**).

(616) 1911 September (No. 12)

Poem (pp. 841–842): *Hymn to Love.*

For notes, see *Emblems of Love* (**5**).

VOICES

(617) 1919 June (Vol. 1, No. 6)

Dramatic poem (pp. 273–281): *In the Dunes.*

For notes, see *Twelve Idyls* (**28**).

THE YEAR'S WORK IN ENGLISH STUDIES

(618) 1924 [Annual for 1923] (Vol. IV)

Article (pp. 1–19): *Literary History and Criticism. General Works.*

(619) 1926 [Annual for 1924] (Vol. V)
Article (pp. 7–25): *Literary History and Criticism. General Works.*

(620) 1932 [Annual for 1930] (Vol. XI)
Article (pp. 7–26): *Literary History and Criticism. General Works.*

UNTRACED PERIODICAL

An article entitled 'The Hundred Geese' on pages 4–5 of an unknown periodical has been examined separated from the periodical. It was probably published in January, 1936, as it is about a painting of the same name, as exhibited in the Chinese Painting Exhibition of December, 1935, to January, 1936, at Burlington House, London.

APPENDIX I
BROADCASTS MADE BY L. A.

BRITISH BROADCASTING COMPANY

All broadcasts were probably transmitted 'live', except where stated.

1925   April 27; Monday (from Leeds–Bradford Programme to all stations, except Belfast; 10.10 to 10.30 p.m.)
Introduction to Poetry.

1925   May 11; Monday (from Leeds–Bradford Programme to all stations; 10.10 to 10.30 p.m.)
Appreciation of Poetry – (3) Sound and Sense.
[This entry, taken from the *Radio Times*, appears to be wrong. It is unknown what the subject of the broadcast was on this date.]

1925   May 25; Monday (from Leeds–Bradford Programme to all stations; 10.10 to 10.30 p.m.)
Appreciation of Poetry – (3) Sound and Sense.

1925   June 8; Monday (from Leeds–Bradford Programme to all stations; 10.10 to 10.30 p.m.)
Imagination.

1925   June 22; Monday (from Leeds–Bradford Programme to all stations; 10.15 to 10.30 p.m.)
The Language of Poetry.

1925   July 6; Monday (from Leeds–Bradford Programme to all stations; 10.16 to 10.30 p.m.)
The Value of Poetry.

1926   January 8, Friday (from London station to 'High-Power Programmes', Daventry only; 2.45 p.m. +)
A special broadcast for schools for demonstration purposes. Subjects – wild animals, French music, and poetry.
[L. A. is not mentioned in the *Radio Times*. He broadcast only part of this programme, which lasted from 2.35 to 3.30 p.m.]

1926   March 5, 12, 18, 26; all Friday (from Leeds–Bradford Programme only; 3.30 to 4.00 p.m.)
Talks to Schools: . . . Greek Mythology [1 to 4]

BRITISH BROADCASTING CORPORATION

1927   June 16; Thursday (from Leeds–Bradford Programme to all stations; 7.27 to 7.45 p.m.)

Victorian Poetry – What is Victorianism?

1927   June 23; Thursday (from Leeds–Bradford Programme to all stations; 7.25 to 7.45 p.m.)
Victorian Poetry – Tennyson and Browning.

1927   June 30; Thursday (from Leeds–Bradford Programme to all stations; 7.28 to 7.45 p.m.)
Victorian Poetry – Pre-Raphaelites.

1927   July 7; Thursday (from Leeds–Bradford Programme to all stations; 7.27 to 7.45 p.m.)
Victorian Poetry – Spasmodics and Rebels.

1927   July 14; Thursday (from Leeds–Bradford Programme to all stations; 7.28 to 7.45 p.m.)
Religious Poets.

1927   July 21; Thursday (from Leeds–Bradford Programme to all stations; 7.27 to 7.45 p.m.)
Victorian Poetry – Doubt and Experiment.

1927   October 9; Sunday (from Leeds–Bradford Programme to all stations; 5.20 to 5.30 p.m.)
Tales from the Old Testament. Nathan rebuking David, 2 Samuel xii, 1–25.

[L. A. is not mentioned in the *Radio Times*.]

1930   April 22; Tuesday (from the National Programme to all stations, except London and Midland regions; 9.25 to 9.45 p.m.)
Rupert Brooke.

[This broadcast was published in its entirety in *Hommage a Rupert Brooke*, q.v. (**120**), and a reduction was published in the *Listener*, q.v. (**255**).]

1931   August 9; Sunday (from the National Programme to all stations; 8.48 to 8.53 p.m.)

The Week's Good Cause. Appeal in aid of the National Trust for Places of Historic Interest or National Beauty.

1933 January 2; Monday

[An entry in L. A.'s diary suggests he had a recording session with the B.B.C. between 10.30 a.m. and 1.00 p.m. to record him reading some poetry. If these recordings were made, and it seems unlikely that they were, it is probable they were never used.]

1935 October 19; Saturday (from the National Programme only; 7.51 to 8.30 p.m.)

Unrehearsed debate: That flats can solve the housing problem. Proposer, Geoffrey M. Bonmphrey; opposer, Sir Ernest Darwin Simon.

[L. A. is not mentioned in the *Radio Times*. According to the B.B.C. he was the chairman, but it is more likely to have been his brother Leslie Patrick.]

1936 April 23; Thursday (from Regional Programme to all stations, except the National; 2.15 to 3.00 p.m.)

Speeches following the luncheon on the occasion of the Annual Shakespeare Birthday Celebration, from the Concert Hall, Stratford-on-Avon.

[L. A. proposed the toast 'The Immortal Memory'.]

1936 November 20; Friday (from the National Programme only; 11.00 to 11.15 p.m.)

Poetry reading: John Dryden.

[Selected and read by L. A.]

1936 November 24; Tuesday (from Regional Programme to all stations, except the North and National; 4.30 to 4.45 p.m.)

John Dryden.

[This was a recorded repeat of the broadcast given on November 20.]

1937 September 18; Saturday (from the National Programme only; 11.00 to 11.15 p.m.)

Reading of Ben Jonson's Poems.

RADIO PARIS

It is alleged that L. A. broadcast a lecture on Radio Paris in December, 1937, but no trace of any details of this has been found.

APPENDIX II
TABLE OF ITEM NUMBERS IN CHRONOLOGICAL ORDER

The order of the numbers is governed by the accuracy of the dates; the inaccurate dates being listed after the more accurate, i.e. May 3, 1908 is before May (3?), 1908, which in turn is before May, 1908. If two items are published on the same date, they go in item order. 'X' means no month is known for that year. Principal books are in bold type; contributions to books in italics.

1902 June?: 612; Nov.: 613.
1903 May: 614.
1907 Mar.: 254; Sept.: 386; Oct.: 387, 388; Nov.: 547.
1908 Jan.: 548, **1**; Feb.: 549, 201; Mar.: 550; May: 202; July: 551, 203; Aug.: 552, 263–274; Sept.: 275–280, 259, 281–284; Oct.: 285–294, 373, 295, 296; Nov.: 297–299, 553, 300–306; Dec. 307–313, 554, 314, 315.
1909 Jan.: 316–320, 555; Feb.: 321; Mar.: 322, 323; Apr.: 324, 325; May: 326; June: 327, 328, 556, 329; July–Dec.: 330–345.
1910 Jan.: 346, 347; Feb.: 223, 348, 349, 557, 205; Mar.: 389, 350, 390; Apr.: 391, 351, 392, 224, 393; May: 394, 225, 395; June: 396, 397, 226; July: 398, 399, 352; Aug.: 400, 353, 401, 402, 227, 403, 228, 404; Sept.: 229, 354, **3**; Oct.: 230, 355; Nov.: 405–408, 356, 409; Dec.: 231, 357, 410.
1911 Jan.: 232, 411; Feb.: 412, 233, 358; Mar.: 413, 414, 234, 415, 359; Apr.: 416, 417, 360, 428, 235, 419; May: 236, 420, 361, 421, 615; June: 362, 422, 423, 237; July: 363, 424, 364, 425; Aug.: **4**, 238, 426, 427, 428; Sept.: 365, 239, 429, 430, 616; Oct.: 431, 432, 366; Nov.?: 367; Dec. **5**, 368, 433.
1912 Jan.: 434–436, 240, 558; Feb.: 437, 438, 241, 439, 440; Mar.: 369, 441–447, 580; Apr.: 581; May: 448–451, 370, 582; June: 452, 453, 371, 372, 242, 249, 583; July: 454–456, 243; Aug.: 244, 457; Sept. 458; Oct.: 459, 460, **6**; Nov.: 245, 461–466, 584; Dec.: 467, **10**, 468, *101*, 585.
1913 Jan.: 469–471, 592; Feb. 472–476, 250; Mar.: 477, 478, 246, 479–482, 576; Apr.: 483–485; May: 486–490; June: 491–496, 207; July: 497–499; Aug.: 500–504, 216; Sept.: 505, 506, 577; Oct.: 507–509, **12**, 510–512; Nov.: 513–516; Dec.: 517.

1952   Apr.: **41.**
1958   X: **34.**
1961   Jan.: **35.**
1962   May: **604.**
1963   Sept.: **27.**
1964   July?: **36;** Dec.: **7.**
1965   Feb.: **42.**
1966   X: **43.**
?   X: **37.**

INDEX

References in italics are to page numbers

155

George, Stephan, 231
George, W. L., 518
Georgian Poetry, 101, 102, 103, 104
German Frankness, 605
Gibbs, Linda, 18
Gibbs, Philip, 421
Gibson, Wilfrid Wilson, 40, 122, 225, 561, 563, 574, 604, *132, 133*
Gilchrist, R. Murray, 430
Gill, Maud, 18
Gillman, Gurner, 551
Gilman, Lawrence, 321
Glover, William, 539
Godfrey-Faussett, Mabel, 551
Goethe, J. W. von, 313
Goldie, V., 571
Gooch, G. P., 565, 601
Good, Irene, 10
Gordon, Jan, 381
Gordon, Kenneth, 18
Gore-Booth, Eva, 552
Gorell, Lord, 248
Gorst, Mrs. Harold, 551
Gosse, Edmund, 376, 553
Gott, Barbara, 20
Gould, George M., 244, 277
Graham, Kenneth, 308
Granville-Barker, H., 126
Gray, Andrew, 271
Great Names, 107
Great Victorians, The, 123
Green Christmas, A, 315
Greg, W. W., 126
Gregory, Lady, 18
Gregynog Festival, 39
Gretton, R. H., 15
Grierson, Francis, 490
Griffiths, D., 18
Gurnhill, J., 569
Gwatkin, Catherine, see Abercrombie, Catherine
Gwynn, Stephen, 119

Haines, W. Ribton, 18
Haldane, Charlotte, 565, 601
Haldane, J. B. S., 565, 596, 601

Hall, W. Winslow, 431
Ham and Eggs, 28, 30, 218
Hamer, S. H., 286
Hanray, Lawrence, 18
Happy Ending, The, 296
Harding, Ellison, 551
Hardy, Thomas, 6, 7, 8, 9, 12, 106, 133, 222, 378, 560, 588
Hare, Maurice Evan, 436
Harecourt, James, 18
Harris, Frank, 495
Harris, George W., 114
Harris, Robert, 20
Harris, Ruth, 10
Harrison, J. R. de W., 18
Hartley, L. Conrad, 440
Hastings, Lord, 565, 601
Headlam, Cecil, 227, 401
Headlam, Walter, 227, 401
Hearnshaw, F. J. C., 127
Heine, Heinrich, 230
Herbertson, Agnes Grozier, 427, 437
Herelle, Roland, 120
Herford, C. H., 215, 519
Herford and International Literature, 215
Hermann, F., 370
Herrick, Robert, 498
Hewlett, Maurice, 110, 229, 327, 579
Hichen, Robert, 416
Hickmott, Arthur, 235
Hield, Robert, 300, 309, *95, 105*
Highway, The, 93
Hilton, A. H., 20
Hilton-Bailey, I., 18
Hodgkin, R. H., 565
Hodgson, William Hope, 449
Hokku: Colours in Herefordshire, 40
Holding, T. H., 267
Holford, William, 20
Holland, A. K., 20
Holles, Philip, 18
Holmes, Edmond, 572
Holtby, Winifred, 596
Home University Library, The, 477
Homer, 110